GINORMOUS
JOKE
BOOK
FOR KIDS!!!
AND THE
GROWNUPS WHO LOVE THEM!

SMITH
FREEMAN
Publishing

*The Ginormous Joke Book for Kids
and the Grownups Who Love Them!*

Cover design by Kim Russell | Wahoo Designs

ISBN 978-1-7378946-4-3

CONTENTS

1

LET'S LAUGH WITH THE ANIMALS

What do you call a shy alligator
who likes to wear vests?

A private in-vesti-gator.

Why did the little boy bring his pet skunk to school?
For show and smell.

What happened when two silkworms had a race?
They ended up in a tie.

How do snails fight?
They slug it out.

After they went shopping,
what did one flea say to the other flea?
*"Do you want to walk home,
or should we take the dog?"*

Zoo Keeper: "Do you have any questions?"
Boy: "Where are the otters?"
Zoo Keeper: "On the otter side of the zoo."

Teacher: "Why do bears hibernate
and sleep for six months?"
Student: "Who would dare wake them up?"

Why aren't koalas considered to be real bears?
Because they don't have the right koala-fications.

What should you do
if you find a tiger in your bed?
Go sleep on the couch.

How can you tell if
there's a rhinoceros in your refrigerator?
The door won't close.

What color socks to bears wear?
They don't wear socks. They prefer to go bare-footed.

Why didn't the skunk buy anything at the mall?
He only had one cent and it was bad.

What happened when a duck, a skunk, and a deer went for dinner at a restaurant and it was time to pay?
The skunk didn't have a scent, and the deer didn't have a buck, so they put the meal on the duck's bill.

First snake: "Are we poisonous?"
Second snake: "I don't know. Why'd you ask?"
First snake: "I just bit my lip."

Girl #1: "Did you know it takes four sheep to make a sweater?"
Girl #2: "No. I didn't even know sheep could knit!"

What do you get when you cross a porcupine and a turtle?
A slow poke.

Where do squirrels store their food?

In the pan-tree.

What kind of vehicles do skunks drive?

Odor-cycles.

Boy #1: "Is it true that an alligator won't bother you if you're carrying a flashlight?"

Boy #2: "It depends on how fast you're carrying the flashlight!"

Hiker #1: "Look, there's a baby snake!"

Hiker #2: "How can you tell it's a baby?"

Hiker #1: "You can tell by its rattle."

What do you call a rabbit that's really cool?

A hip hopper.

Where do sheep
get their hair cut?
At the baa baa shop.

How do you stop a skunk from smelling?
You hold his nose.

What is a frog's favorite drink?
Croak-a-cola.

Which animal knows its A-B-Cs?
An alpha-bat.

What's the game mice love to play?
Hide and squeak.

What do you call a flea that
rides from place to place on a dog?
An itch-hiker.

What did the caterpillar
do when he got out of jail?
He turned over a new leaf.

Where do yellow jackets go when they get sick?
To the waspital.

What's black and white and red all over?
A sunburned zebra.

What did the judge say when
the skunk walked into the courtroom?
"Odor in the court!"

What side of a polar bear has the most fur?
The outside.

What did the father buffalo say
when his boy went off to summer camp?

"Bison."

Why do pandas like old movies?
Because they're in black and white.

What happened to the frog
that swallowed the firefly?
It croaked with delight.

What do you call a rabbit with fleas?
Bugs Bunny.

What do penguins wear on their heads?
Ice caps.

What do you get if you cross a parrot with a shark?
A bird that will talk your ear off.

Boy #1: "What do you get when
you cross a bear and a skunk?"
Boy #2: "I don't know, but it shouldn't have
a problem getting a seat on a bus."

Why did the ants do gymnastics
on the top of the jelly jar?
Because the lid said, "Twist to Open."

What do you get when you
cross a centipede with a parrot?
A walky-talky.

What kind of footwear
do frogs prefer?
Open-toad shoes.

Pretend you're in Africa and a lion is chasing you.
What should you do?
Stop pretending!

Why can't you play hockey with pigs?
They always hog the puck.

Why couldn't the leopard escape from the zoo?
Because he was always spotted.

2
RIDDLES, RIDDLES, AND MORE RIDDLES

What does a clock do when it gets hungry?

It goes back four seconds.

Why did the house painter go to the clothing store?
He wanted a second coat.

Why did the bubble leave the bath?
He was looking for his pop.

What did the mommy needle
say to the baby needle?
"It's way past your thread-time."

Which is braver: a stone or a stump?
The stone, because it's a little boulder.

What do you call a guy named Lee
who changed his name?
Formerly.

What did the mop say to the bucket?

"Are you okay? You look a little pail."

What word becomes shorter
when you add two letters to it?

Short.

What nails do carpenters hate to hit?

Fingernails.

What do you get a man who has everything?

A burglar alarm.

Where does a boat go when it gets sick?

To the dock!

Why did the bicycle fall over?
Because it was two-tired!

What did Cinderella say
when her photos didn't show up on time?
"Someday my prints will come."

Why was the belt arrested?
Because it held up some pants.

Which hand is it better to write with?
Neither hand. It's best to write with a pencil.

Why did the man run around his bed?
To catch up on his sleep.

Why would Snow White make a great judge?
Because she was the fairest in the land.

How do you make a fire with two sticks?
Make sure one of them is a match.

What do you call a king who's only 12 inches tall?
A ruler.

What's the tallest building in the world?
A library, because it has so many stories.

Why did the boy sit on his watch?
He wanted to be on time.

How do scientists
freshen their breath?

With experi-mints.

What kind of dress can't be worn?

An address.

What did one candle say to the other candle?

"I'm going out tonight."

What runs but doesn't get anywhere?

A refrigerator.

What stays on the ground but never gets dirty?

A shadow.

What did the bald man say
when he got a new comb?

"I'll never part with this."

Which will burn longer: a match or a candle?

Neither. They'll both burn shorter.

What do you get if you cross
a bird, a car, and a dog?

A flying car-pet.

What time is it when the clock strikes 13?

Time to fix the clock.

What did the left hand say to the right hand?

"What does it feel like to always be right?"

What did the scarf say to the hat?

"You go on a head. I'll hang around."

What can you put
in a barrel of water to make it lighter?
A hole.

What do firefighters put in their soup?
Firecrackers.

How do billboards talk?
They use sign language.

Why are police officers the
strongest people in the world?
Because they can hold up traffic with a single hand.

Why couldn't the pirate play cards?
Because he was sitting on the deck.

How many pairs of shoes does a jet plane need?
Enough for 30,000 feet.

What happens once in a month, twice in a moment,
but never in a hundred years?
The letter M.

What do you call a spoiled tightrope walker?
An acro-brat.

Why did the confused woman smear lipstick on her
forehead?
She wanted to make-up her mind.

Why was the fire hydrant not working?
Because it was dehydrated.

What did the
molecule's mom say
to him every morning?
"Up and atom!"

What do you salt but never eat?
An icy sidewalk.

If you say my name,
I'm already gone. What am I?
Silence.

Where do superheroes shop?
At the supermarket.

What did the elevator say to his doctor?
"I think I'm coming down with something."

Why did the tightrope walker go to the bank?
To check his balance.

How many sides does a circle have?
Two: the in-side and the out-side.

What does Cinderella wear to the beach?
Glass flippers.

Why did the detective stay in bed?
Because he wanted to stay under-cover.

3

MERRILY THEY ROLL ALONG: THINGS THAT GO VROOOOM!

What happened to the wooden car with wooden tires and a wooden engine?

It wooden go.

Driver #1: "When I got into my car this morning, the steering wheel, the radio, and the pedals were missing. So I called the police."

Driver #2: "What did they say?"

Driver #1: "They told me I was in the back seat."

What type of cars do elves drive?

Toy-otas.

What has three letters and starts with g-a-s?

A car.

Where would a car go if it had a dent?

To a dentist.

What do you call a song that's played on a car radio?

A car tune.

What do you call a motorcycle
that loves to tell jokes?
A Yamahaha.

What is the most tired part of your car?
The exhaust pipe.

What do you call a car that's covered in leaves?
An autumn-obile.

Why did the man have to repair his car horn?
Because it didn't give a hoot.

What do you call the life story of a car?
An auto-biography.

Where do cars swim?

In a car pool.

What kind of bus has two floors and says, "Quack?"

A double-ducker.

How do you make antifreeze?

Steal her blanket.

What do you get when you put a car in the oven?

A hot rod.

Why did the traffic light turn red?

*You would too if you had to change
in the middle of the street.*

What did the car wheels say
after a cross-country trip?
"We're tired out!"

Where do race car drivers go
to wash their clothes?
To the laundry vroom.

How do locomotives hear?
Through their engineers.

What would happen if
every citizen owned a pink car?
Then we'd be living in a pink carnation.

How do you get a locomotive to obey you?
You train it.

What kind of locomotive
needs a tissue?

Ah-choo-choo train.

What did the jack say to the car?

"Can I give you a lift?"

What's a train's favorite sport?

Track.

What's the difference between
a bus driver and a cold?

One knows the stops and the other stops the nose.

Boy #1: "My dad just built a car out
of washing machine parts."
Boy #2: "Where's the car?"
Boy #1: "He took it out for a spin."

What happened to the
train engineer after he retired?

He got sidetracked.

What kind of truck does a ballerina drive?

A toe truck.

What did one car call to the other?

**"You look familiar.
Haven't I bumped into you before?"**

Where do antique Volkswagens go?

To the old Volks home.

What part of a car causes the most accidents?

The loose nut behind the wheel.

Boy #1: "Did you hear about the string of robberies
at the high-rise parking lot?"
Boy #2: "Yeah. It was wrong on so many levels."

4
SCHOOL DAZE

Teacher: "What do George Washington, Abraham Lincoln, and Christopher Columbus have in common?"

Boy: "They were all born on a holiday."

Did you hear about the kid with good penmanship?
He got straight A's.

Teacher: "What did they do at
the Boston Tea Party?"
Student: "I don't know. I wasn't invited."

Teacher: "You've got your shoes on the wrong feet."
Boy: "But these are the only feet I've got!"

Student #1: "Which planet is closest to us?"
Student #2: "Venus?"
Student #1: "No way, silly; it's Earth."

What is the difference between
a schoolteacher and a train?
**The teacher says spit your gum out and the train
says, "chew chew chew."**

Teacher: "Can you name four seasons?"
Student: "Salt, pepper, vinegar, and sugar."

What do you call someone who studies hives?
A B-student.

Teacher: "Sometimes, I think you don't
hear a word I say."
Boy: "What?"

Student: "Would you punish me for
something I didn't do?"
Teacher: "Of course not. Why do you ask?"
Student: "Because I didn't do my homework."

What do you call an arithmetic teacher who can
make numbers disappear?
A mathemagician.

Teacher: "We start class at 8:30 sharp."
Boy: "If I'm not there, go ahead
and start without me."

Teacher: "If you had $10 in one pocket and $20 in
another pocket, what would you have?"
Student: "Another person's jeans!"

Student #1: "Have you heard the story
about the broken pencil?"
Student #2: "No. How does the story go?"
Student #1: "Never mind. It's pointless."

Boy: "Our English teacher is really old."
Girl: "Why do you say that?"
Boy: "She said she used to teach Shakespeare."

Teacher: "Where is your homework?"
Student: "A ghost ate it."
Teacher: "I can see right through that excuse."

Why did the boxer
go to the library?
He wanted to hit the books.

Teacher: "Suppose you have ten candy bars and you ate nine of them. What do you have now?"
Student: "A stomachache!"

Teacher: "Name two pronouns."
Student: "Who, me?"
Teacher: "Correct!"

Teacher: "Your socks are mismatched."
Boy: "I know. I've got another pair at home just like 'em."

Why did the clock have to go to the principal's office?
It tocked too much.

Teacher: "The word 'inquisitive' means curious. Can you spell it?"
Student: "Sure I can: I–T."

Teacher: "How many letters are in the alphabet?"
Student: Eleven.
Teacher: "No. There are 26 letters in the alphabet. How did you get eleven?"
Student: "T-H-E-A-L-P-H-A-B-E-T."

Voice on the Phone: "I'm afraid my boy won't be at school today."
Principal: "Who's calling?"
Voice on the Phone: "My mom."

During a test, one student passed a note to the kid seated next to him. The note said, "I have absolutely no idea what 'plagiarism' means. Can I copy the answer from you?"

Why did the art student flunk his test?
He drew a blank.

Boy #1: "I got 100 in school today."

Boy #2: "That's great. Which class?"

Boy #1: "I got a 50 in math and a 50 in social studies."

Boy #1: "Do you like homework?"

Boy #2: "I like nothing better."

Mother: "What did you learn in school today?"

Daughter: "Not enough. I still have to go back tomorrow."

Teacher: "Can you tell me about the Dead Sea?"

Student: "No. I didn't even know it was sick."

Student #1: "Did you hear about the four new states?"

Student #2: "No. What are they?"

Student #1: "New York, New Jersey, New Hampshire, and New Mexico."

A book just fell on my head,
but I've only got my shelf to blame.

Teacher: "On the last test, you copied
your friends answer."
Student: "How could you tell?"
Teacher: "Because on question #12, he wrote,
'I don't know,' and you wrote, 'Me neither.'"

Teacher: "Joey, come up to the front of the class
and spell 'mouse' on the board."
Joey writes m-o-u-s.
Teacher: "What's on the end?"
Joey: "A tail."

Mom: "Why are you doing so
poorly in history class?"
Boy: "Because the teacher keeps asking about
stuff that happened before I was born!"

Teacher: "What was that loud noise?"
Boy: "My jacket fell on the floor."
Teacher: "Why did your jacket make such a loud noise?"
Boy: "Because I was wearing it when it fell."

What is the world's longest punctuation mark?
The hundred-yard dash.

How did the boat do in school?
It sailed through all its classes.

Teacher: "What was that loud noise I just heard?"
Student: "I'm not sure, but I think it was the chemistry class flunking their exam."

Mother: "Do you know a boy named Tommy Tubbs?"
Son: "Of course I know him. He sleeps next to me in history class."

5
FUN WITH FISH

Which fish is the funniest?

The cartoona.

What fish only swims at night?
A starfish.

What clubs do girl whales like to join?
The Girl Spouts.

What are the easiest animals to weigh?
Fish, because they have their own scales.

What do jellyfish eat for breakfast?
Floatmeal.

What did the boat say to the pier?
"What's up, dock?"

Why did the young fish stay home from school?
He was feeling a little under the water.

What kind of gum do whales chew?
Blubber gum.

Are shellfish warm?
No, they're clammy.

How do you communicate with a fish?
You drop him a line.

What do fish paint with?
Watercolors.

What kind of fish chews bubble gum?
A blowfish.

How does a fish cut through seaweed?
With a sea saw.

What do fish use to calm their babies?
A bassifier.

Why do fish love libraries?
Because that's where they can find bookworms.

How much rent did the one crab charge
the other crab to stay in his sandcastle?
Five sand dollars.

Why do fish in the ocean
stay so healthy?

*Because they always get
plenty of "Vitamin Sea."*

How come Batman and Robin
never caught any fish?

Because Robin kept eating all the worms.

What cruises around the ocean floor
and holds lots of people?

An octobus.

Why are some fish at the bottom of the ocean?

Because they dropped out of school.

Why are fish bad at basketball?

They're afraid of the nets.

What do you call a whale that can't keep a secret?
A blubber-mouth.

Where do sailors take baths?
In a tubmarine.

Why should you never tell a joke while ice fishing?
Because the ice might crack up.

Where does the army keep its fish?
In a tank.

What's the easiest way to scoot across the ocean floor?
Take a taxi crab.

What's the difference between a fish and a guitar?

You can't tuna fish.

What do you get when you cross
a whale and a tree?

A fish stick.

Which sea creature can add big numbers?

An octoplus.

Why did the ocean scream?

It found crabs in its bed.

What do you call a fish with no eye?

Fsh.

When is a boat the cheapest?
When it's a sale boat.

Whose picture is on the sand dollar?
President George Washing-tuna.

What did the fisherman
say to the magician?
"Pick a cod, any cod."

Why should you never pick
a fight with an octopus?
Because they're always well-armed.

Why didn't the fisherman
believe the talking fish?
Is sounded fishy.

What do pelicans eat?
Anything that fits the bill.

How do fish wash themselves?
In the river basin.

Why are the other fish sick and tired
of listening to the whales?
Because the whales are always spouting off.

When can a fishing net hold water.
When the water is frozen.

What's the most popular game show for fish?
Whale of Fortune.

Did you hear about the captain who had to park a very big boat at a very small dock?

He was under a lot of pier pressure.

Does a dolphin ever do something by accident?

No, they do everything on porpoise.

Game warden: "Didn't you see the no-fishing sign?"
Boy: "I'm not fishing, sir. I'm just teaching these worms how to swim."

Boy #1: "Did you give your goldfish water today?"
Boy #2: "No. They didn't finish the water I gave them yesterday."

Why did the dolphin cross the bay?

To get to the other tide!

What happened when the
shark became famous?
He turned into a starfish.

How do you make a goldfish old?
Take away the g!

Where do fish keep their money?
In a river bank!

What subject do some fish take in schools?
Debate.

6

FUNNY DOCTORS AND DAFFY DENTISTS

Patient: "Doctor, I think I'm shrinking."
Doctor: "Calm down. You'll just have
to be a little patient."

Doctor: "Why do you look so tired?"
Patient: "I knew I had a doctor's appointment, so I stayed up all night studying for my blood test."

Patient: "Doctor, my ear is ringing. What should I do?"
Doctor: "Answer it."

Patient: "Doctor, I have a terrible problem. I think I'm invisible!"
Doctor: "Who said that?"

Man #1: "I've been seeing spots all day."
Man #2: "Did you see the eye doctor?"
Man #1: "No, just spots."

Doctor: "You're in perfect health. Your pulse is as steady as clockwork."
Patient: "Maybe you should take your thumb off my wristwatch."

A patient went to see an eye doctor. The doctor asked, "Do you want your eyes checked?" "No thanks," said the patient, "I'd rather leave them solid blue."

Patient: "I think I'm losing my memory."
Doctor: "When did it start?"
Patient: "When did what start?"

Doctor: "Nurse, did you take the patient's temperature?"
Nurse: "No. Is it missing?"

Patient: "Doctor, last night I had a bad dream. I dreamed there was a door with a sign on it. I pushed and pushed, but the door wouldn't open."
Doctor: "That's interesting. What did the sign say?"
Patient: "Pull."

Patient: "Doctor, I think I broke my arm in two places."
Doctor: "Well, don't go back to those places."

Patient: "Doctor, I have a weak back."
Doctor: "When did you first notice the problem?"
Patient: "Oh, about a week back."

Patient: "Doctor, do you make house calls?"
Doctor: "Yes, but the house has to be very sick."

Boy: "Doctor, doctor, my sister is invisible."
Doctor: "What sister?"

Why did the king go to the dentist?
To get his teeth crowned.

Why did the pie crust go to the dentist?
Because it needed a filling.

Patient: "Doctor, my Legos are broken.
What do you recommend?"
Doctor: "Plastic surgery."

When does a doctor get mad?
When he runs out of patients.

What did one tonsil say to the other tonsil?
"Get dressed up, the doctor is taking us out!"

What did the judge say to his dentist?
**"Do you swear to pull the tooth, the whole tooth,
and nothing but the tooth?"**

Patient: "Doctor, I get heartburn every time I eat birthday cake."

Doctor: "Next time, try taking the candles off."

Patient: "Doctor, I have yellow teeth, what should I do?"
Dentist: "Wear a brown tie."

Doctor #1: "Did you hear about the guy whose left side fell off?"
Doctor #2: "No. How is he doing?"
Doctor #1: "He's all right now."

Mother: "Do you feel better now that you've gone to the dentist?"
Boy: "I sure do. He wasn't in."

What did the dentist say to the computer?

"This won't hurt a byte."

Scientist #1: "I just discovered that exercise kills germs!"

Scientist #2: "But how do you get a germ to exercise?"

Patient: "Doctor, there must be something wrong with me. Sometimes, I think that I'm a dog."

Doctor: "Sit down on the couch and we'll talk about it."

Patient: "But I'm not allowed on the couch."

Patient: "Doctor, everybody keeps ignoring me."

Doctor: "Next!"

What do dentists call x-rays?

Toothpicks.

What does a dentist do on a roller coaster?

He braces himself.

What do you call a dentist in the army?
A drill sergeant.

What did the doctor say to the frog?
"You need a hoperation."

What makes the tooth fairy so smart?
It's the wisdom teeth.

Why did the flower go to the dentist?
It needed a root canal.

Why should you never try to lie
to an x-ray technician?
Because they can see right through you.

Why did the man whisper every time
he went to the drug store?
He didn't want to wake the sleeping pills.

What do you call a small wound?
A short cut.

What do you call a group of
dentists who work together?
A drill team.

Why did the boy refuse to go to the dentist?
Somebody told him the dentist was boring.

Why did the doctor keep his bandages in the fridge?
Because he wanted to use them for cold cuts.

When is your veterinarian
the busiest?

When it's raining cats and dogs.

Patient: "Doctor, I'm worried.
Last night I dreamed
I was a muffler."
Doctor: "What's to bad about that?"
Patient: "I woke up exhausted."

Patient: "Doctor, I keep thinking I'm a pat of butter,
and I know it's crazy, but I don't want to stop."
Doctor: "Why can't you stop?"
Patient: "Because now I'm on a roll."

When do doctors perform best in school?
When they give it their best shot.

Patient: "Doctor, I've got a problem. Whenever I fall
asleep, I kick the blanket off my bed. Can you help me?"
Doctor: "Don't worry. I'm sure
I can help you re-cover."

Patient: "Doctor, I have a carrot growing out of my ear."
Doctor: "How could that have happened?"
Patient: "I have no idea. I planted celery."

Patient: "Doctor, I sleepwalk every night."
Doctor: "Congratulations. You're living the dream."

Patient: "Help me, Doctor. I think I'm going to die in 59 seconds!"
Doctor: "I'll be with you in a minute."

Patient: "Doctor, I keep thinking that I'm a bridge. What's come over me?"
Doctor: "So far, it's been three cars, two trucks, and a bus."

Patient: "Doctor, can you give me something for a headache?"

Doctor: "Here's a medical dictionary. Read it for an hour and you'll have a headache."

Patient: "Doctor, every time I go to a new restaurant, I feel like I've been there before."

Doctor: "Are you having déjà vu?"

Patient: "No, I'm having chicken."

Patient: "Doctor, sometimes I think I'm sailing on an ocean made out of orange soda? What's wrong with me?"

Doctor: "You're having a Fanta-sea."

Patient: "Doctor, I keep thinking I'm a church bell."

Doctor: "Take two aspirin, and if it doesn't work, give me a ring in the morning."

Dentist #1: "I won Dentist of the Year. They gave me a big trophy?"
Dentist #2: "You're lucky. When I won it, they only gave me a little plaque."

Patient: "Doctor, when I look up at the sky, it looks purple instead of blue."
Doctor: "Don't worry. It's just a pigment of your imagination."

Patient: "Doctor, I think I'm Napoleon."
Doctor: "How long have you felt that way?"
Patient: "Ever since the Battle of Waterloo."

Doctor: "I gave you specific instructions. I told you to take your medicine every night after your bath. Why haven't you done it?"
Patient: "It's not my fault. By the time I finish drinking the bath, there's no room left for the medicine."

Patient: "Doctor, I've had a bad stomachache ever since I ate a dozen oysters yesterday."
Doctor: "Did they smell bad when you took them out of their shells?"
Patient: "What do you mean 'took them out of their shells?'"

Patient: "I feel like I'm about to turn into a sheep."
Doctor: "How does that make you feel?"
Patient: "Baaaaaad."

Patient: "Doctor, I'm afraid I'm going to turn into a dog."
Doctor: "Sit!"

Doctor: "I really need a break. So, who's my next appointment?"
Nurse: "The Invisible Man."
Doctor: "Tell him I can't see him right now."

7

LAUGHS FROM OUTER SPACE

Astronaut #1: "What's that thing in your frying pan?"
Astronaut #2: "I don't know. It's an unidentified frying object."

Boy #1: "I tried to watch the moon for 24 straight hours."
Boy #2: "Did you make it?"
Boy #1: "No, I watched it for 12 hours and then I had to call it a day."

What do aliens eat for breakfast?
Flying sausages.

What was the first animal in space?
The cow that jumped over the moon.

How do you have a successful solar system party?
You plan-et!

When is the moon the heaviest?
When it's full!

Why is outer space like professional basketball?
They both have shooting stars.

What blooms in outer space?
Sunflowers.

What are astronomers' three
favorite days of the week?
Saturnday, Sunday, and Moonday.

What do planets like to read?
Comet books.

Why did the Martian get a ticket?
He forgot to pay his parking meteor.

When did the moon go broke?

When it got down to its last quarter.

What is an astronomer's
favorite key on the keyboard?

The space bar.

How do you stop an astronaut's baby from crying?

You rocket.

Why didn't the rocket have a job?

Because it had already been fired.

Why couldn't the astronaut
book a hotel room on the moon?

Because it was full.

How does an astronaut
hold up his pants?

With an asteroid belt.

What is the clumsiest thing in outer space?

A falling star.

How did Mary's little lamb get to the moon?

On a rocket sheep.

How does the man in the moon cut his hair?

Eclipse it.

What happens when an astronaut drops his sundae?

He ends up with an ice-cream float.

What holds up the sun?

Sunbeams.

Why didn't the sun go off to college?
Because it already had thousands of degrees.

Why do hamburgers always
taste better in outer space?
Because they're meteor.

A black hole is the tunnel at the end of the light.

How do astronauts tie their shoes?
With astro-knots.

Where do aliens keep their coffee cups?
On flying saucers.

How many ears does Captain Kirk have?

Three: a left ear, a right ear, and a final front-ear.

If athletes get athlete's foot,
what do astronauts get?

Missile toe.

How did the astronaut keep his rocket warm?

He brought along a space heater.

What did the astronomer see in the middle of
Jupiter?

The letter i.

How does the solar system hold up its pants?

With the asteroid belt.

What do stars do when they want a snack?

They take a bite out of the Milky Way.

What kind of music does the Sun like?

Neptunes.

What do you call a very sad UFO?

A crying saucer.

What kind of life did they find on Pluto?

Mickey found fleas.

What did the alien's mother say
when he returned home?

"Where on Earth have you been?"

How did Darth Vader know what
Luke Skywalker got him for Christmas?
He felt his presents.

What do you call a call a robot that
takes the long way home?
R2 Detour.

Living on Earth can be expensive, but at least
you get a free trip around the Sun every year.

What did Jupiter say to Saturn?
"Give me a ring sometime."

The kid was up all night wondering where
the sun had gone.
The next morning it dawned on him.

8

YOU MUST BE JOKING

What happened to Mickey Mouse
when he fell into the bathtub?

He came out squeaky clean.

Boy #1: "I was asked to be in a movie."

Boy #2: "So did you do it?"

Boy #1: "No way! I didn't want to be in a cast."

Camper #1: "This is a dogwood tree."

Camper #2: "How can you tell?"

Camper #3: "By its bark."

Passenger #1: "I just flew in from Buffalo."

Passenger #2: "Boy, your arms must be tired!"

Boy #1: "A cowboy rides into town on Friday. He stays there three days and leaves on Friday. How does he do it?"

Boy #2: "I don't know. How?"

Boy #1: "His horse is named Friday."

Why are elevator jokes so good?

Because they work on so many different levels.

Why does Waldo wear stripes?
Because he doesn't want to be spotted.

What do you call an apology that's
written in dots and dashes?
Re-morse code.

Who makes the best exploding underwear?
Fruit of the Boom.

Why do AA batteries always feel left out?
**Because every time you buy a new gadget,
it says "Batteries not included."**

What's green, has webbed feet,
and is hard to see through?
Kermit the Fog.

Why do historians call it "the Dark Ages?"

**Because back in those days,
there were so many knights.**

Where should you send your shoes for the summer?

Boot camp.

How can you tell if a cat burglar
has been in your house?

Your cat is missing.

Why did the pirate put a chicken on
top of his treasure chest?

Because eggs marks the spot.

What did the pirate say when his wooden
leg got stuck in a snowbank?

"Shiver me timbers!"

Who was the plumpest knight
at King Arthur's Round Table?

Sir Cumference.

What did the pirate say
on his 80th birthday?

"Aye, matey."

What do you call a princess
who keeps falling down on the ice?

Slipping Beauty.

Who carves wooden figures
and lives in the ocean?

The Whittle Mermaid.

Why did Rapunzel loved going to parties?

Because she liked to let her hair down.

What was Humpty Dumpty's least favorite season?

Fall.

Why did the Texas cowboy buy a dachshund?

*Because somebody told him
to get a long little doggie.*

What does an envelope say when you lick it?

Nothing. It just shuts up.

Why did the boy throw a pat
of butter out the window?

He wanted to see a butter-fly.

What kind of paper makes you itch?

Scratch paper.

What person is always in a hurry?

A Russian.

Who can marry lots of wives and still be single?

A minister.

When is a chair like a soft fabric?

When it's satin.

What is bought by the yard and worn by the foot?

A carpet.

What can you hold without touching it?

A conversation.

What is the difference between a hill and a pill?
A hill is hard to get up and a pill is hard to get down.

Boy #1: "I got a part-time job at the factory."
Boy #2: "What do you make?"
Boy #1: "Mostly mistakes."

Girl #1: "How did you like the Liberty Bell?"
Girl #2: "It's not all it's cracked up to be."

Boy #1: "I eat birthday cake every day."
Boy #2: "Isn't that a little bit excessive?"
Boy #1: "Somewhere out there somebody's having a birthday, and what kind of person would I be if I ignored it?"

What kind of underwear do reporters wear?
News briefs.

9

IT'S A LIVING: JOKES ABOUT JOBS

Boy #1: "I'd like to take over the clown's job."
Boy #2: "Those are big shoes to fill."

Who never gets paid for a day's work?

A night watchman.

Why did the comedian go broke?

Because his jokes didn't make any cents.

What do postal workers do when they get mad?

They stamp their feet.

What did the lawyer name his daughter?

Sue.

What do lawyers wear to court?

Lawsuits.

Who earns a living by driving
his customers away?

A taxi driver.

How did the banker start
every bedtime story?

"Once upon a dime..."

Boy #1: "I want to get paid to sleep."
Boy #2: "That would be a dream job."

What do you call a pirate who
constantly skips school?

Captain Hooky.

What do you call a lawyer's house?

A legal pad.

Why did the policeman stop the ball of yarn?
Because it was weaving in and out of traffic.

Why did the pioneers cross America
in covered wagons?
**Because they didn't want to wait
fifty years for a train.**

Which famous inventor was also a practical joker?
Ben Pranklin.

What did Ben Franklin say when he
flew a kite in a lightning storm?
He didn't say anything. He was too shocked.

Old carpenters don't retire.
They just lumber around.

What were the
spy's favorite shoes?
His sneakers.

Where do comedians go to lunch?

The laugh-a-teria.

What kinds of gum do scientists chew?

Ex-spearmint gum.

Why did the truck driver put a clock under his seat?

He wanted to work overtime.

What do you call a happy cowboy?

A jolly rancher.

How do florists make a living?

By petaling their merchandise.

Why do magicians do so well in school?

They're good at trick questions.

What was the reporter doing at the ice cream shop?

Getting a scoop.

What do you call a knight who gives up too soon?

Sir Render.

What did the policeman say to his shirt?

"You're under a vest!"

Who can shave ten times a day
and still have a beard?

A barber.

What's the difference between a jeweler
and the captain of a ship?

One sees the watches and the other watches the seas.

Who's richer: the butcher, the baker,
or the candlestick maker?

The baker. He's got the most dough.

What did the policeman say to his upset stomach?

"Halt! You're under a vest."

Where do butchers dance?

At the meatball.

What do you call a person who mows
the grass at a baseball stadium?

A diamond cutter.

What's the difference between
a tailor and a horse trainer?

One mends a tear and the other tends a mare.

What do you call a highly educated plumber?

A drain surgeon.

What do you call an expert on carbonated drinks?

A fizzician.

What is the difference between
a locomotive engineer and a teacher?

One minds the train; the other trains the mind.

What do you need to know
if you want to be a real estate agent?

Lots.

Why can't people keep
secrets at a bank?

**Because there are
too many tellers.**

Did you hear about the bankrupt origami business?

It folded.

What person always falls down on the job?

A paratrooper.

What is the difference between
a gardener and a billiard player?

One minds his peas; the other minds his cues.

Why do electricians have so many friends?

Because they know how to make good connections.

Why do barbers make such good cab drivers?

They know all the shortcuts.

Boy #1: "What do you want to be when you grow up?"
Boy #2: "Inspecting mirrors is a job I could really see myself doing."

Boy #1: "My dad just quit his job at the doughnut factory."
Boy #2: "Why?"
Boy #1: "He was fed up with the hole business."

Man #1: "My boss accused me of acting like a monkey at work."
Man #2: "How'd you take it?"
Man #1: "I almost choked on my banana!"

The best thing about being a tree-trimmer is that when you do a good job, they let you take a bough.

Did you hear about the human cannonball?
He got fired.

Boy #1: "My sister was a barista at a coffee shop, but she had to quit."

Boy #2: "What happened?"

Boy #1: "She couldn't stand the daily grind."

Employee: "A guy just ran out of the store with three sweaters, two shirts, and one pair of pants."

Manager: "Why didn't you run after him?"

Employee: "They were my pants."

What do you call a hero who wears a mask, rides a horse named Silver, and works at a bank?

The Loan-Arranger.

Copilot: "Sir, we're now going faster than the speed of sound."

Pilot: "What?"

10

LAUGHS FROM THE WORLD OF SPORTS

I couldn't figure out why the baseball
keptgetting bigger...

Then it hit me.

What do you do with whiny baseball player?
Take him out to the bawl park.

What is a cheerleader's favorite color?
Yeller.

What is the hardest part about skydiving?
The ground.

Lifeguard: "Why are you doing the backstroke?"
Swimmer: "Because the sign says that
I shouldn't swim on a full stomach."

When is cross-country skiing easy?
When you live in a very small country.

When is a baseball player like a spider?

When he catches a fly.

Which sport is always in getting into trouble?

Bad-minton.

Why was Cinderella a bad soccer player?

Because she always ran away from the ball.

What is a boxer's favorite drink?

Punch.

Why is tennis such a loud game?

Because each player raises a racquet.

What's the quietest sport?
Bowling.
You can hear a pin drop.

Why did the baseball player leave
in the middle of the game?

**Because the manager
told him to run home.**

What did the baseball glove
say to the baseball?

"Catch you later."

Why did the baseball manager
call the police?

**Because a player on the
other team stole a base.**

Why do porcupines always win their games?

Because the always have the most points.

Why did the basketball player go to jail?
Because he shot the ball.

What does a ball do when it stops rolling?
First it stops. Then it looks round.

What is harder to catch the faster you run?
Your breath.

How do basketball players keep cool during a game?
They sit near the fans.

What's the sport where you sit down
going up and stand up going down?
Skiing.

Where do joggers take a bath?
In running water.

What can you serve but never eat?
A tennis ball.

What runs around a baseball field but never moves?
The fence.

What did the football coach say
to the broken vending machine?
"I want my quarter back!"

What kind of stories do basketball players tell?
Tall tales.

What did the baseball cap name his daughter?

Hattie.

Why did the football player bring rope to the game?

Because he wanted to tie the score.

Why did the weightlifter hate his job?

Because he worked with dumbbells.

What do Olympic sprinters eat before a race?

Nothing. They fast.

Why did the baseball player go
into the recording studio?

To get a big hit.

What kind of ice cream do tennis balls like best?

Soft serve.

What's the difference between a world-class sprinter and a locomotive engineer?

**One trains to run
and the other runs a train.**

What's the best advice to give
a young baseball player?

**If at first you don't succeed,
try playing second base.**

Which takes longer to run: from first base
to second or from second base to third?

**It takes longer from second to third because
there's a shortstop in the middle.**

What do you call an Italian referee?
A Roman umpire.

What kind of person plays basketball in designer
clothes, a Rolex watch, and Gucci loafers?
A gym dandy.

What does a baseball umpire do before he eats?
He brushes off his plate.

The track star had a fear of hurdles,
but he got over it.

Boy #1: "My football coach invented
a new position just for me."
Boy #2: "Cool. What is it?"
Boy #1: "Coach says I'm a drawback."

11
FUN WITH FOOD

Carrot: "I had a nightmare last night.
I dreamed I was in a salad."
Lettuce: "What's so bad about that?"
Carrot: "I tossed all night!"

What do you have if you have 18 apples in one hand and 13 apples in the other hand?

Very big hands.

What is every magician's favorite candy?

Twix.

How much did the pirate pay for his corn?

A buccaneer.

What did the egg do when it saw the frying pan?

It scrambled.

Why did the colander retire?

It just couldn't take the strain anymore.

Why do the French eat snails?
Because they don't like fast food.

What's yellow and hangs from an apple tree?
A confused banana.

How do you know when
it's too hot in the chicken coup?
When the chickens start laying hard boiled eggs.

Who makes shoes for fruit?
Apple cobbler.

What did the hot dog say when
he finished first in the hundred-yard dash?
"I'm a wiener!"

When are apples sold in the seafood department?

When they're crab apples.

Why did the girl smear peanut butter on the road?

To go with the traffic jam.

Why did the potato cross the road?

Because it saw a fork up ahead.

What happens when all the chefs go on strike?

You have a cook-out.

Who led the apples to the bakery?

The Pie Piper.

What do you call a stolen yam?

A hot potato.

What's a pirate's favorite vegetable?

Arrrrrrrtichoke.

What did the frog order at McDonald's?

Flies and a diet croak.

Why did the cantaloupe wade into the ocean?

It wanted to be a watermelon.

What do you call a potato
that's watching a football game?

A spec-tater.

Who writes nursery rhymes and squeezes oranges?

Mother Juice.

What kind of bagel can fly?

A plain bagel.

Why did the chef get arrested?

Because he beat the eggs, whipped the crème, and mashed the potatoes.

How do you make an apple turnover?

You push it down the hill.

What do young sweet potatoes wear to bed?

Their yammies.

What kind of pizza do they serve
at the bottom of the ocean?

Deep dish.

Why did the hamburger have so many friends?
Because he was the life of the patty.

Why did the dinner roll enter the fashion show?
Because it wanted to be a roll model.

What happened to the toaster
when the boy put jelly in it?
It jammed.

What did the pork chop say to the steak?
"Nice to meat you."

What do you call cheese that's not yours?
Nacho cheese.

How do you fix a pizza?
With tomato paste.

What did the baby corn say to the mommy corn?

"Where is pop corn?"

What do you call a nice french fry?

A sweet potato.

Where were the first potatoes fried?

In Greece.

What two things can you not have for breakfast?

Lunch and dinner.

What's the best thing to put into a pie?

Your teeth.

What kind of nuts sneeze the most?

Cashews!

What is green and sings?

Elvis Parsley

What candy do you eat on the playground?

Recess pieces.

Why don't you starve in a desert?

Because of all the "sand which" is there.

What do you call a peanut in a spacesuit?

An astronut!

Where do you go to learn
how to make a banana split?

Sundae school.

Why did the banana go to the hospital?

Because it wasn't peeling well.

What do you call two banana peels?

A pair of slippers.

What do you call a fake noodle?

An impasta.

What kind of sandwiches do grizzly bears like?

Growled-cheese sandwiches.

What do you get when a hen
lays an egg on the roof?
You get an eggroll.

If a carrot and lettuce ran a race, who would win?
The lettuce, because it's a head.

Girl #1: "Sometimes reading makes me hungry."
Girl #2: "When?"
Girl #1: "When I'm reading a menu."

Boy #1: "How do you eat your soup?"
Boy #2: "With my right hand."
Boy #1: "That's funny. I use a spoon."

A tomato, some lettuce, and some water were in a
race. The water was running; the lettuce was ahead;
and, the tomato was trying to catch up.

12

ANIMALS DO THE FUNNIEST THINGS

Why did the marsupial from Australia
get fired on his first day at work?

Because he wasn't koala-fied.

Why did the pig get hired at the restaurant?
Because he was really good at bacon.

What do you get when you cross a goat and a squid?
Billy the Squid.

What did the alpaca say when he
got fired from his job on the farm?
"Alpaca my bags."

What do you get when you
cross a bear and a skunk?
Winnie the Pew.

What do you call a bear caught in a rainstorm?
A drizzly bear.

Where do animals go when they lose their tails?
They can go to any retail store.

What's white, furry, and shaped like a tooth?
A molar bear.

What do you call a sheep covered in chocolate?
A candy baaaaa.

What fur do you get from a skunk?
As fur away as possible.

What did the preacher skunk
say to his congregation?
"Let us bow our heads and spray."

What do you call a sheep in toe shoes?
A baaaaaalarina.

What do you call a three-foot aardvark?
A yard-vark.

What do you get when you
cross a pig and a centipede?
Bacon and legs.

What kind of books do skunks read?
Best-smellers.

Young Skunk: "Mom, why can't I have a
chemistry set for my birthday?"
Mother Skunk: "Because it would
stink up the house."

What do well-behaved lambs
say to their mothers?

"Thank ewe."

What do you call an ant that was mailed
in from another country?

An important.

What is every squirrel's favorite opera?

The Nutcracker.

What happens if you give the king
of the jungle an Xbox?

You get a lion gamer.

What did one firefly say to the other
firefly when his light went out?

"Can you give me a jump start? My battery is dead."

What do you call a sick crocodile?
An illigator.

What do you get when you cross a cow and a duck?
Milk and quackers.

Why don't ants get sick?
They have anty bodies.

What looks like a snake, swims, crawls, and honks?
An automob-eel.

Why don't flies fly through screen doors?
Because they don't want to strain themselves.

Which animals didn't come on the ark in pairs?

Worms. They came in apples.

What is the strongest animal?

The snail, because it carries its house on its back.

What do people in England call little black cats?

Kittens.

If dogs have fleas, what do sheep have?

Fleece.

What would happen if you
accidentally swallowed a frog?

You might croak.

How did the bashful turtle
finally get a date?

He finally came out of his shell.

In what kind of home do the buffalo roam?
A dirty one.

How is a pig like a horse?
**When a pig is hungry, he eats like a horse.
And when a horse is hungry, he eats like a pig.**

How should you treat a baby goat?
Like a kid.

What did the mother kangaroo say
when her baby went missing?
"Help! Somebody just picked my pocket!"

How did the panda do in school?
He bearly made it.

If you're surrounded by four lions,
two tigers, a hippo, a leopard,
and five wild horses, what should you do?
Wait until the merry-go-round stops and get off.

What do you get if you cross
a skunk and an eagle?
A bird that stinks to high heaven.

What do you get when you
cross a lion and a parrot?
**I don't know, but if it asks for a cracker,
you'd better give it to him.**

Why are Kentucky horses so kind?
Southern horsepitality.

What do you get if you
cross a parrot with a shark?
A bird that will talk your ear off.

Why did the fly fly?
Because the spider spied 'er.

What was the snail doing on the highway?
About 1 mile a week.

How do bed bugs get around?
They itch-hike.

Why couldn't the butterfly go to the dance?
Because it was a mothball.

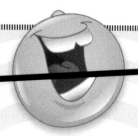

13

LAUGHING WITH MOTHER NATURE

What happened when the
red ship sank in the Black Sea?

The crew was marooned.

What do two oceans do when they meet?
Nothing. They just wave.

What washes up on itty-bitty beaches?
Microwaves.

What did the tree say to the wind?
"Leaf me alone."

Who got to the beach first,
the big wave or the little wave?
In the end, they were tide.

What type of tree is most likely to get sick?

A sick-amore.

What do you get when you throw
a box of books into the ocean?

A title wave.

How does a tree draw a person?

It makes a stick figure.

Which United States president
liked nature the most?

Tree-adore Roosevelt.

Which plant is best at gymnastics?

The tumbleweed.

Who cleans the bottom of the ocean?
A mer-maid.

If you breathe oxygen during the day,
what do you breathe at night?
Nitrogen.

What has no fingers but has many rings?
A tree.

Where does the snowman keep his money?
In the snow bank.

Which Great Lake do ghosts like best?
Lake Eerie.

What did the tree wear to the pool party?

Swimming trunks.

Why is the ocean floor so sandy?

Because there's a shortage of mermaids.

Why are rivers lazy?

Because they never get out of their beds.

What does the ocean eat for breakfast?

Boatmeal.

What are mountain climbers' favorite books?

Cliffhangers.

What should you do if you get trapped on top of an iceberg?

Just chill.

What do you call a funny mountain?

Hillarious.

Why is lava red hot?

**Because if it were cold and white,
it would be snow.**

What can go through water and not get wet?

Sunlight.

Which mountain is always sleeping?

Mount Ever-rest.

What kind of tree can you fit into your hand?

A palm tree.

What's the hairiest tree?

A fir tree.

How do trees get on the internet?

They log on.

What was the tallest mountain
before Mt. Everest was discovered?

Mt. Everest.

Where do trees keep their money?

In branch banks.

How many acorns grow on the average pine tree?

None. Pine trees don't have acorns.

Why do canyons get fat?
Because they gorge themselves.

Why did the tree surgeon change into his pajamas?
He was invited to a lumber party.

Why are mountains so funny?
Because they are hill-areas.

How did the rainbow do in school?
It passed with flying colors.

Why couldn't the iceberg give a speech?
It froze.

What month do trees fear most?

Sep-timber!

What do you call a jungle filled
with highly intelligent trees?

A brain-forest.

Mountain Climber #1: "I just climbed the
highest mountain in the world."
Mountain Climber #2: "Everest?"
Mountain Climber #1: "Yeah, about
every 100 feet or so."

Boy #1: "I saw a picture of the Amazon River.
It's amazing."
Boy #2: "I know, but I still can't believe
they named it after a web page."

14

OH, THE PLACES YOU'LL GO IN THE GOOD OLD USA

Which state do sheep like best?

Alabaaaama.

What state is on a horse?

Maine.

Which state is married?

Mississippi.

Which state has the most streets?

Road Island.

What is a birthday candle's favorite state?

Wish-consin.

Knock, knock.
Who's there?
Alaska.
Alaska who?

Alaska expert and get back to you on that.

What do you call a hippie's wife?

Mississippi.

Why is Alabama the smartest state?

Because it's got 4 A's and only one B.

Which state has the most okra?

Okra-homa.

What is round on both ends and hi in the middle?

Ohio.

Which state is warmest in the winter?

Fur-ginia.

Which city always needs a compass?

Lost Angeles.

What state has 2,000 pounds of dirty laundry?

Washington.

Why did they name it Wyoming?

Wy not?

What state has the most acorns?

Oaklahoma.

What clothes did Delaware?

A New Jersey.

Which state has the
smallest drinks?

Mini-soda.

Which state is the best place
to celebrate Thanksgiving?
Ken-turkey.

What stands over New York Harbor
and sneezes all day?
The Achoo of Liberty.

Why did the chocolate lovers
move to Alaska?
They heard the state was full of mousse.

What is the capital of Louisiana?
L.

What state comes packed in water?

Tuna-see.

What's the feeling you get when
you're sad about leaving Alabama?

Alabummer.

Which state is the place where
everybody seems happy?

Merry-land.

Which state is the easiest place to catch a cold?

Mass "achoo" setts.

What did Tennessee see?

The same thing Arkansas.

Which state has the most hogs?

New Hamshire.

Which state has the best smelling breath?

Vermint.

Which state has the most dogs,
cats, hamsters, and canaries?

Petsylvania.

What is a cowboy's favorite state?

Cow-a-fornia!

Boy #1: "Did you know that they
made a sequel to Oregon?"
Boy #2: "What did they name it?"
Boy #1: "Moregon."

15

LET'S LAUGH ABOUT MATH

Why couldn't 16 marry 17?

Because they were both under 18.

Boy #1: "If I gave you two goldfish
and my sister gave you two more,
how many would you have?"
Boy #2: "I'd have six."
Boy #1: "You're wrong! Two plus two equals four."
Boy #2: "But I already have two goldfish."

Why did the little kids like learning addition?
They thought it was a real plus.

What happened when the student
didn't understand the math problem?
The teacher summed it up for him.

What is the most mathematical part of speech?
The add verb.

Why was 6 afraid of 7?

Because 7 ate 9.

If two's a couple and three's a crowd,
what are four and five?

Nine.

What did Zero say to Eight?

"Nice belt!"

How many feet are in a yard?

It depends on how many people are standing in it.

Why is the number 9 like a peacock?

Because without its tail, its nothing.

What kind of insects love math?

Arithma-ticks.

If there are four apples
and you take away three,
how many do you have?

You took three apples, so you've got three.

What did one math book say
to the other math book?

"Don't bother me. I've got my own problems!"

What gets smaller when
you turn it upside down?

The number 9.

Which king loved fractions?

Henry the one-eighth.

Which member of royalty is best at math?

The Count.

Why was the math student so bad at decimals?

He couldn't get the point.

Mathematician #1: "What's your favorite
type of numbering system?"
Mathematician #2: "I, for one,
like Roman numerals."

Why is it dangerous to do arithmetic in the jungle?

Because if you add 4 + 4 you get ate.

What happened when twenty-nine
and thirty got into a fight?

Thirty-one.

Four out of three people find fractions confusing.

How do you divide 11 potatoes
equally between 7 people?
First, you mash the potatoes...

What do you call a number that can't sit still?
A roamin' numeral.

What do you say to the guy who invented zero?
"Thanks for nothing."

Parallel lines have so much in common
that it's a shame they'll never meet.

16

FUN WITH OUR FINE FEATHERED FRIENDS

Which bird never goes to the barber shop?

A bald eagle.

Girl #1: "I know someone who thinks he's an owl!"
Girl #2: "Who?"
Girl #1: "Make that two people."

Why are pigeons so good at baseball?
Because they always know how to get home.

When does a teacher carry birdseed to school?
Whenever she has a parrot-teacher conference.

Why does a flamingo lift up one leg?
Because if it lifted up both legs it would fall over.

What subject do owls like to study?
Owl-gebra.

Why do seagulls like to live by the sea?

Because if they lived by the bay, they'd be bagels.

What kind of birds always stick together?

Vel-crows.

When is a duck not a duck?

When it's afloat.

When is the best time to buy a bird?

When it's going cheep.

What's every bird's favorite chocolate?

Nest-lees.

What's the main difference between
a duck and George Washington?

**One has a bill on his face
and the other has his face on a bill.**

What do you call a bird that goes
to the North Pole for the winter?

A brrrrrrrd.

What time did the duck wake up?

At the quack of dawn.

What do you call a bird that smells bad?

A foul fowl.

Why did the duck become a spy?

**_Because he was good
at quacking codes._**

What do you call a crate filled with ducks?

A box of quackers.

What sound does a hummingbird make when it's thinking?

Hummmmmm.

Why are flamingos always happy?

Because they're never blue!

Do baby birds go to flight school?

No, they just wing it.

Which bird lifts the most weight?

A crane.

What has feathers and says, "I'm a turkey?"

A talking turkey.

What type of key can't open any doors?

A tur-key.

What's a duck's favorite meal?

Soup and quackers.

Why did the duck hire a detective?

He wanted to quack the case.

How do baby ducklings get out of their shells?

They eggs-it.

Why did the duck cross the road?
To prove that he wasn't chicken.

Which bird always needs cheering up?
A blue bird.

Why is a dime like a turkey sitting on a fence?
Head's on one side, tail's on the other.

What do birds get when they sing in the rain?
Wet.

What does a duck wear when he gets married?
A duxedo.

What did the bird-doctor do for his patient?

He gave him tweetment.

Why do birds fly north in the summer?

Because they don't know how to drive.

What do you call a hot, noisy duck?

A fire-quacker.

What is a bird's favorite game?

Fly-and-seek.

What do you call a man who
has a seagull sitting on his head?

Cliff.

What do you call an owl that
performs magic tricks?
Hoo-dini.

Why were the momma owl and the daddy owl
worried about their teenage owl?

Because it didn't seem to give a hoot about anything.

What do you call a fast duck?

A quick quack.

Why do turkeys gobble?

Because they never learned table manners.

What's the difference between
the bird flu and the swine flu?

**For the bird flu, you need tweetment.
For the swine flu, you need oinkment.**

How do you stop geese from speeding?

Goose bumps.

What do you call a crazy duck?

A wacky quacky.

What happened to the turkey who got in a fistfight?

He got the stuffing knocked out of him.

What kind of bird do criminals hate?

A stool piggeon.

Where do owls learn best?

Night school.

Boy #1: "My aunt's giant parrot just died."
Boy #2: "How is she taking it?"
Boy #1: "Actually, it's a big weight
off her shoulders."

17
FUN WITH MAN'S BEST FRIEND

What did the dog say when
he sat down on sandpaper?

"Ruff!"

Boy: "A dog bit my leg this morning."

Nurse: "Did you put anything on it?"

Boy: "No, he liked it plain."

What did the spy name his dog?

Snoopy.

Where do dogs park their cars?

In a barking lot.

Boy #1: "Did you like the story about the dog that ran three miles just to pick up a stick?"

Boy #2: "No, I thought it was a little far-fetched."

Why did the dog get kicked out of the choir?

He kept barking off key.

Boy #1: "My dog chases everybody on a bicycle. What should I do?"
Boy #2: "Take away his bicycle!"

Which dog can catch a football?
A golden receiver.

What do you give a dog with a fever?
Mustard. It's the best thing for a hot dog.

Boy #1: "My dog plays chess."
Boy #2: "He must be a really smart dog."
Boy #1: "He's not that smart. He's only beaten me a couple of times."

What kind of dog is best with babies?
A baby setter.

Where do dogs refuse to shop?

At the flea market.

What happened when the dog ate the clock?

It got lots of ticks.

What dog washes her hair in the shower?

A shampoodle.

What does a dog call his daddy?

Paw.

Boy #1: "My dog is lazy."
Boy #2: "How lazy?"
Boy #1: "He's so lazy that he
only chases parked cars."

What goes tick-tock, bow-wow,
tick-tock, bow-wow?

A watch dog.

Pet owner: "My dog is sick. Do you know
a good animal doctor?"
Pet owner's friend: "Nope. All the doctors
I know are people."

Why did the dog make such great grades in school?

He was the teacher's pet.

What do you call a dog who designs dog houses?

A barkitect.

Why did the dog leap for joy?

Joy was his owner.

What's the only kind
of dog that can tell time?
A watch dog.

What is the first thing
a dog learns in school?
The arf-a-bet.

What kind of dog wears a watch?
A clocker spaniel.

What time would it be if you saw
10 dogs chasing a cat up a tree?
10 after 1.

Girl #1: "I like your dog. What kind is it?"
Girl #2: "She's a police dog."
Girl #1: "She doesn't look like a police dog."
Girl #2: "That's because she's undercover."

What kind of dog always runs a fever?

A hot dog!

Why didn't the boxer want to play basketball?

Because he was a boxer.

What do dogs do when they're
tired of watching Netflix?

They press "paws."

Why are dogs bad dancers?

Because they have two left feet.

What do you call a dog magician?

A Labra-ca-dabra-dor.

What is a dog's favorite city?
New Yorkie!

What should you know before
you try to teach a dog a trick?
More than the dog.

Why can dogs scratch wherever they feel like it?
Because they live in a flea country.

Which household cleaner terrifies dalmatians?
Spot remover.

What do you get when you cross a dog and a rose?
A collie-flower.

What do sheepdogs turn into every summer?

Hotdogs.

Why did the bloodhound get fired?

**Because its owner found
out that it had no scents.**

Why did the dog have
splinters in his tongue?

Because he always ate table scraps.

Which holiday do dogs like best?

Howl-o-ween.

Why do dogs run
around in circles?

**Because it's easier than
running around in squares.**

What happened to the dog
that swallowed the firefly?
It barked with de-light.

What's the best treat to give to dogs on Halloween?
Halloweenies.

When is a black dog not a dog?
When it's a greyhound.

Why is it so confusing when a dog barks
and wags its tail at the same time?
Because you don't know which end to believe.

Why couldn't the dog catch its tale?
Because these days, it's hard to make ends meet.

How do dog catchers get paid?
By the pound.

What makes a dog scratch
and laugh at the same time?
The Flea Stooges.

Boy #1: "I spent my entire life savings
on a golden retriever."
Boy #2: "Why'd you do that?"
Boy #1: "They retrieve gold, right?"

Boy #1: "My dog is so bossy."
Boy #2: "How can you tell?"
Boy #1: "It's always barking orders."

18
MUSICAL MUSINGS

Why couldn't the music teacher open the door?

Because his keys were on the piano.

Piano Tuner: "I'm here to tune your piano."

Lady: "But I didn't call you."

Piano Tuner: "No, but your neighbors did!"

What's a plumber's favorite song?

"Singing in the Drain."

Why did the drum take a nap?

It was beat.

Song Writer: "It took me five years
to write this lullaby."

Singer: "Why did it take you so long?"

Song Writer: "It kept putting me to sleep."

When is a tuba good for your teeth?

When it's a tuba toothpaste.

Why is a slippery sidewalk like music?

Because if you don't C-sharp you'll B-flat.

Why are trains and orchestras alike?

They both have conductors.

Why did the girl climb the ladder to sing?

She wanted to reach the high notes.

Farmer #1: "My chickens love classical music."

Farmer #2: "How can you tell?"

Farmer #1: "They keep asking me to play, Bach, Bach, Bach!"

What kind of music do mummies listen to?

Wrap music.

What do you call a cow that
plays a musical instrument?

A moo-sician.

What did the drummer call his twin daughters?

Anna One, Anna Two.

What do musicians do when they lose their beat?

They throw tempo-tantrums.

What bone will a dog never eat?

A trombone.

What kind of music did the Pilgrims play?

Plymouth Rock.

Why did people like dancing when
the Vegetable Band played?

Because their music had a good beet.

What musical instrument is usually
used in the bathroom?

A tuba toothpaste.

What kind of music do balloons hate?

Pop.

Why did the broken trombone
go to the playground?

Because he heard it had a new slide.

What would happen if a piano fell on you?

You would B-flat!

What makes pirates
such good singers?
They can hit the high C's.

Why did the burglar break into the music store?

Because he wanted the lute.

When their band director left,
why did the high schoolers go crazy?

Because they didn't know how to conduct themselves.

Why did the guitar get mad?

Because it was sick and tired of being picked on.

What kind of paper makes music?

Rapping paper.

Why did the piano player keep banging
his head against the keyboard?

Because he wanted to play by ear.

How do you make a bandstand?

You take away their chairs.

Why was the phonograph
record always nervous?

You would be, too, if you lived on spins and needles.

Boy #1: "My friend Phil is so good at
playing the harmonica that they put
him in charge of his own orchestra."

Boy #2: "What's the name of the orchestra?"

Boy #1: "The Philharmonica."

Musician #1: "I just played a gig in Hawaii."

Musician #2: "How did it go?"

Musician #1: "Great. People were
dancing in the isles."

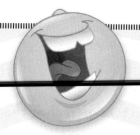

19
FUN WITH DINOSAURS

Boy #1: "I wish I had enough money
to buy a dinosaur."
Boy #2: "What would you do with a dinosaur?"
Boy #1: "Who wants a dinosaur?
I just want the money!"

Student #1: "What family does T. Rex belong to?"
Student #2: "I don't think any families in our neighborhood have one."

What did the dinosaur say after
he rear-ended another car?
"I'm so-saurus!"

Why did dinosaurs walk so slowly?
Because running shoes hadn't been invented yet.

Where did the T. rex buy things?
At a dino-store.

What do you call a T. rex wearing
cowboy boots and a 10-gallon hat?
Tyrannosaurus Tex.

How can you tell if there's a
T Rex in the refrigerator?

**There's a green tail sticking out of the
door and your lunch meat is missing.**

Why was the dinosaur afraid to go to the library?
Because his books were millions of years overdue.

What do you call a dinosaur
whose shoes are too tight?
A My-feet-are-saurus.

What do you call a dinosaur that's
about to about to tell a funny joke?
Pre-hysterical.

What is a dinosaur's favorite meal?
Macaroni and trees.

What should you do if you find
a dinosaur in your bed?
Find somewhere else to sleep.

Which dinosaur has the biggest vocabulary?
A Thesaurus.

What do you call a paranoid dinosaur?
A Do-you-think-he-saurus.

What do you call a sleeping dinosaur?
A dino-snore.

What do you get if you cross a pig with a dinosaur?
Jurassic Pork.

What do you get when dinosaurs crash their cars?
Tyrannosaurus wrecks.

20
FUN WITH THE CALENDAR

Which month has 28 days?

All of them!

Which month do soldiers hate most?

The month of March.

What's the best season to jump on a trampoline?

Spring time.

Why was 2019 afraid of 2020?

Because they had a fight and 2021.

Why are people so tired on April 1st?

Because they just completed a 31-day March.

When is the best time to buy a thermometer?

In the winter. That's when it's the lowest.

What are the strongest days of the week?
Saturday and Sunday. The rest are weak-days.

What is a lumberjack's favorite month?
Sep-TIMMMMMBER!

Did you hear about the
two guys who stole a calendar?
They each got six months.

Can February March?
No, but April May.

Why does Humpty Dumpty love autumn?
Because he always has a great fall.

What's the best day to go to the beach?
Sun-day.

Boy #1: "I think calendars are
going out of style."
Boy #2: "Why?"
Boy #1: "Because I think their
days are numbered."

Why is history the fruitiest subject?
Because it's full of dates.

How far is it from March to June?
A single spring.

21

A FUNNY THING HAPPENED ON THE WAY TO THE CLASSROOM

Why are kindergarten teachers so great?

Because they know how to make the little things count.

Why did the boy take his father's
credit card to school?
Because he wanted extra credit.

Why did the jump rope get suspended from school?
It wouldn't stop skipping class.

What kind of school makes you drop out
before you can graduate?
Paratrooper school.

What is a teacher's favorite country?
Expla-nation.

What did the teacher put on top of her pizza?
Graded cheese.

Teacher: "You did well on your homework. That's an excellent essay for someone your age."

Student: "How about for someone my mother's age?"

Boy #1: "I'm surprised that my teacher gave me homework on the very first day of school."

Boy #2: "Why are you surprised by that?"

Boy #1: "I just thought it would take me a lot longer to start falling behind."

Teacher: "If your coat had six pockets, and you found a twenty-dollar bill in every pocket, what would you have?"

Student: "Somebody else's coat."

Why did the girl bring her mother's credit card to school?

She wanted to get extra credit.

Teacher: "Where's the English Channel?"
Student: "I have no idea. We don't get cable."

Why was the boy's report card so wet?
It was under C-level.

How did Bob the Builder do on his final exam?
He nailed it.

Teacher: "If there were 10 flies on my desk, and I swatted one, how many would be left?"
Boy: "One. The dead one."

Son: "I hate school. The teachers don't like me and the kids bully me."
Mother: "I don't care. You've still got to go."
Son: "Give me two good reasons."
Mother: "First, you're 40 years old, and second, you're the principle."

What happened when the teacher tied all her students' shoelaces together?

They had a class trip.

Why was the broom late for school?

It over swept.

Teacher: "What was the moral of last night's reading assignment?"
Boy: "Don't read it."

Student #1: "I went to the library, but the librarian couldn't help me."
Student #2: "Why not?"
Student #1: "She was totally booked."

Why is school like a shower?

One wrong turn and you're in hot water.

What do you call a teacher who always calls her students by the wrong names?

Miss Pronounce.

Why was the piece of paper on the bulletin board so scared?

It was always under a tack.

What happened when the class clown held the door open for the little girl?

She thought it was a nice jester.

Teacher: "What's the plural of mouse?"
Girl: "Mice."
Teacher: "What's the plural of baby?"
Girl: "Twins."

Why were the teacher's eyes crossed?

Because she couldn't control her pupils.

Boy #1: "The origami teacher
at our school just quit."
Boy #2: "Why?"
Boy #1: "Too much paperwork."

Boy #1: "I was late to school again today."
Boy#2: "What did you tell the teacher?"
Boy #1: "I told her I sprained my ankle."
Boy #2: "That was a lame excuse."

Student #1: "At school, tomorrow is
Jamaican hairstyle day."
Student #2: "I'm dreading it."

Student #1: "My teacher asked me to
write a story about my life."
Student #2: "How did it go?"
Student #1: "At first I was nervous,
but then I composed myself."

Sign on the school bulletin board:
"Today's meeting of the Procrastinator's Club
has been postponed indefinitely."

What do you call a student who doesn't like math class?
A calcu-hater.

Boy #1: "I just finished a book about
how planes are held together."
Boy #2: "What'd you think?"
Boy #1: "It was riveting."

Teacher: "Class, I have a question,
and I want you to answer at once. What's 9 + 5?"
Class: "At once!"

Teacher: "Are you good at math?"
Student: "Yes and no."
Teacher: "What do you mean 'yes and no?'"
Student: "I mean yes I'm no good at math."

What is a pronoun?
A noun that gets paid.

Father: "Would you like help with your homework?"
Son: "No thanks. I'd rather get it wrong by myself."

What happens when kids flunk
their coloring-book tests?
They need a shoulder to crayon.

Teacher: "If I lent your father $10 and he
agreed to pay me back $1 a month,
how much would he owe me in 5 months?"
Boy: "He'd owe $10."
Teacher: "I'm afraid you don't know
much about arithmetic."
Boy: "I'm afraid you don't know
much about my father."

What did the lobster give his teacher?
A crab apple.

Teacher: "Your homework looks like it was written in your mother's handwriting."
Student: "I can explain. I used her pen."

Student: "Excuse me, but I don't think I deserved a zero on my homework."
Teacher: "I don't either, but it was the lowest grade I could give."

Teacher: "Can you tell the rest of the class what happened when the apple fell on Isaac Newton's head?"
Student: "He finally understood the gravity of the situation."

Why did the schoolteacher fall in love with the janitor?
Because he swept her off her feet.

22

FUN WITH LETTERS AND WORDS

What do you get when you put M and T together?

Nothing...it's empty.

Knock, knock.
Who's there?
Spell
Spell who?
W-H-O.

How do you spell "enemy" in three letters?
F-O-E.

What starts with a P, ends with an E,
and has a million letters in it?
Post office.

What do you find in the middle of nowhere?
The letter H.

Why were U, V, W, X, Y,
and Z late to the tea party?
Because they always come after T.

What do you call an X that just took a bath?

A clean X.

Why is the letter G scary?

Because it turns a host into a ghost.

How do you make notes out of stone?

You rearrange the letters.

Why couldn't the pirate learn the alphabet?

Because he always got lost at C.

There is one in every corner and
two in every room. What is it?

The letter O.

Which letters are not in the alphabet?

The ones in the mail.

Which is the longest word in the dictionary?

"Smiles," because there are miles between each "s."

If this word is pronounced wrong it's right and if it's pronounced right is wrong. What is it?

Wrong.

How do you make the word "One" disappear?

Just add the letter G and it's Gone.

How can you spell jealousy with just two letters?

NV.

Why is dark spelled with a "k" instead of a "c?"

Because you can't "c" in the dark.

If the alphabet goes from A to Z,
what goes from Z to A?

A zebra.

How do you make varnish vanish?

Take away the R.

How do you make a witch itch?

Take away the W.

What word allows you to take away
two letters and get one?

Alone.

What word starts with "e" and ends with "e" but
only has one letter in it?

Envelope.

How do you make seven even?

Take away the S.

From what word can you take away
the whole and still have some left?

Wholesome.

One of the words in this sentence is misspelled.
Which one is it?

Misspelled.

Words to live by:
If at first you don't succeed, don't try skydiving.

23
FUN ON THE FARM

Farmer: "How did you get that bump on your nose?"

Boy: "I bent down to smell a brose."

Farmer: "There's no 'b' in rose."

Boy: "There was in this one!"

What happens when you feed
gun powder to a chicken?

An egg-splosion.

Farmer: "How much bird seed should I buy?"
Store clerk: "How many birds do you have?"
Farmer: "I don't have any birds,
but I want to grow some."

Why did the chicken go to jail?
Because he was using fowl language.

Why do cows go to New York?
To see the moosicals!

Why did the farmer spend hours
talking to his cornfield?
They were all ears.

What happened to the little chicken
who kept misbehaving at school?

She got eggspelled.

How do you fit more pigs onto your farm?

Build a sty-scraper.

Why shouldn't you tell a secret on a farm?

**Because the potatoes have eyes
and the corn stalks have ears.**

Why did the chicken cross the playground?

To get to the other slide.

What's a farmer's favorite car?

A cornvertable.

Why did Mozart get rid of his chickens?

Because they kept saying, "Bach, Bach, Bach."

How did the rancher count his cattle?

On a cow-culator.

What made the chicken good at basketball?

He made his fowl shots.

What kind of math can you teach to cattle?

Cow-culus.

How do you describe an excellent farmer?

Someone who is out standing in his field.

What did the farmer say to his cows at midnight?

"It's pasture bedtime."

What is a cow's favorite day?

Moo-years Day!

How does a rooster wake himself up every morning?

He sets his alarm clock-a-doodle-do.

What do cows do for entertainment?

Go to the moo-vies.

Why did the pig have ink all over his face?

He had just come out of a pen.

What do you call a
cow that won't give milk.
A milk dud.

What's the most important use of cowhide?

To hold the cow together.

Why did the farmer dump his crop on the ground?

He wanted there to be peas on Earth.

Why did the rooster cross the road?

Because it was the chicken's day off.

What did the pig use to wash its hooves?

Ham-sanitizer.

What's worse than finding a worm in your apple?

Finding half a worm in your apple.

What do you call an elevator that only pigs can use?

A pork lift.

What did the chicken say when
it laid a square egg?

"Ouch!"

How do you arrest a pig?

You use hamcuffs.

What did the farmer give his
family for Valentine's Day?

Hogs and kisses.

Why did the chicken cross the road,
jump in the mud, and cross the road again?

Because it was a dirty double-crosser.

Why do cows wear cowbells?
Because their horns don't work.

How do pigs behave when they
go on spring break?
They go hog-wild.

What are the hardest beans to grow in a garden?
Jelly beans.

Where do chickens dance?
At the fowl ball.

What did the pig say on the
hottest day of the summer?
"I'm bacon!"

Why did the rooster call in sick?

He had the cock-a-doodle flu.

What do you call a pig who knows karate?

A pork chop.

What do you call a horse that
is too antsy to stay in the barn?

Unstable.

Why did the hens refuse to lay any more eggs?

They were sick and tired of working for chicken feed.

How do you keep your milk from getting sour?

Just leave it in the cow.

What disease do rodeo riders
get from riding wild horses?

Bronc-itis.

What's the poorest plant?

A vine, because it can't support itself.

How do you take a pig to the hospital?

In a hambulance.

Why did the chickens run away from home?

Because they were tired of being cooped up.

What's every cow's favorite city?

Moo York.

How do pigs talk to each other?

They use swine language.

How did the farmer repair his pants?
With cabbage patches.

Why did the chicken go just
halfway across the road?
She wanted to lay it on the line.

What do you call a cow who mows your grass?
He's a lawnmooer.

Why did the farmer decide
to plant car parts in his garden.
He wanted a bumper crop.

If you pamper your cow too much,
what do you get?
Spoiled milk.

Why do pigs have the best writing instruments?
Because their pins never run out of oink.

Why do gardeners hate weeds?
If you give weeds an inch, they'll take a yard.

How do hens dance?
Chick to chick.

Why do bulls always pay with credit cards?
Because they love to charge.

Why shouldn't you ever tell a secret to a pig?
Because they're all squealers.

Who conquered half the world while
laying eggs along the way?
Attila the Hen.

What do you call a sleeping bull?
A bulldozer.

Why did the farmer think
he was strongest man in the world?
Because he raised an 500-pound pig.

Did you hear about the chicken
who invented a computer?
All you have to do is point and cluck.

Where do young cows eat lunch?
In the calf-ateria.

Why don't scarecrows have any fun?
Because they're all stuffed shirts.

Where do pigs go to get clean?
The hogwash.

What kind of magazines do cows like best?
Cattlelogs.

Why did the pig run away from home?
**He thought all the other pigs
were taking him for grunted.**

What do you call a cow with a twitch?

Beef jerky.

Why did the cowboy ride the bull?

It was too heavy to carry.

What does a calf become after it's six months old?

Seven months old.

What do you call a cow on a trampoline?

A milkshake.

Why are barns so noisy?

The goats have horns.

How do cows text?

They use e-moo-jis.

What was the farmer's favorite part of school?

The field trips.

Why shouldn't you cry if your
cow falls out of the treehouse?

Because there's no use in crying over spilled milk.

Why did the barn fall down?

It was unstable.

The farmer had 199 cows in his field,
but when he rounded them up, he had 200.

Farmer #1: "I prefer to have my milk churned."
Farmer #2: "Why?"
Farmer #1: "It's butter that way."

Farmer #1: "I wanted to grow some herbs,
but I didn't do it."
Farmer #2: "Why?"
Farmer #1: "I couldn't find the thyme."

Farmer #1: "Last night a strong wind blew
down my lemon tree."
Farmer #2: "That was a bitter blow."

Farmer #1: "One of my chickens is sick."
Farmer #2: "That's too bad. What does
your chicken have?"
Farmer #1: "People-pox."

24
FROM YOUR HEAD TO YOUR TOES

What did one eyeball say to the other eyeball?

"Between you and me something smells."

What's the smartest part of the eye?

The pupil.

Why is your nose in the middle of your face?

Because it's the scenter.

If parents have grown-up knees, what do their children have?

Kid-knees.

When is a bump like a hat?

When it's felt.

How do eyes communicate with each other?

They use contacts.

What can you hold in your right hand
but not in your left hand?

You left elbow.

What kind of cap do you always take with you
but never put on your head?

A kneecap.

What has a neck but no head?

A bottle.

What kind of flower grows on your face?

Tulips.

What tastes better than it sounds?

A tongue.

What's the most musical bone?

The trom-bone.

What makes music in your hair?

A head band.

When are eyes not eyes?

When the wind makes them water.

What smells the best at dinner?

Your nose.

Why can't your nose be 12 inches long?

Because then it would be a foot.

25

KIDS SAY THE CRAZIEST THINGS

Boy #1: "Can you answer one
simple question for me?"
Boy #2: "Sure."
Boy #1: "Thanks."

Boy #1: "Did you take a bath yesterday?"
Boy #2: "No. Why? Is one missing?"

Boy #1: "For her birthday, my sister wanted something with diamonds in it."
Boy #2: "So what did you get her?"
Boy #1: "A deck of cards."

Girl #1: "I've been swimming since I was six years old."
Girl #2: "You must be tired."

Boy #1: "My friend Tommy's mother has five children. Their names are Penny, Nickel, Dime, and Quarter. What's the fifth child's name?"
Boy #2: "Dollar?"
Boy #1: "No. His name is Tommy."

What is a baby's motto?
If at first you don't succeed cry, cry again!

Boy #1: "Can I share your sled?"
Boy #2: "Sure. We'll go half and half."
Boy#1: "Thanks! I'll take it for the downhill, and you can have it for the uphill."

What do kids play when they can't play with a phone?
Bored games.

Girl #1: "Call me over the weekend."
Girl #2: "Okay."
Girl #1: "Got to go. Bye."
Girl #2: "Bye, Over the Weekend."

Boy #1: "I just saw two of my friends walk into a building."
Boy #2: "That's weird. You'd think at least one of them would have seen it."

Why did the boy
take his pencil to bed?

He wanted to draw the curtains.

Boy #1: "Was there ever a time in history when nerds ruled everything?"
Boy #2: "Yeah. I think they called it the Dork Ages."

Girl #1: "What do you get when you cross a rattlesnake with a rose?"
Girl #2: "I don't know, but I wouldn't try to smell it!"

Boy #1: "You ate my potato chips! What kind of person are you?"
Boy #2: "Like you, only not hungry."

Girl #1: "How was your roller-skating lesson?"
Girl #2: "It was hard."
Girl #1: "What was the hardest part?"
Girl #2: "The pavement."

Boy #1: "You've been searching the internet for hours. What on earth are you looking for?"
Boy #2: "My patents told me time is precious. So, I'm looking for better ways to waste it."

Girl #1: "That's a beautiful dress. Did it come from Europe?"
Girl #2: "No, it came from France."

Boy #1: "The tongue-twister champion just got arrested."
Boy #2: "I bet he gets a long sentence."

Boy #1: "Did you hear the story about the champion peacock?"
Boy #2: "No, but I hear it's a beautiful tail."

Girl #1: "I'm going to the Netherlands to shop for clogs."
Girl #2: "Why would you want to go there?"
Girl #1: "Wooden shoe?"

Boy #1: "A big pile of trousers fell out of a truck and landed on the street in front of my house."
Boy #2: "What did you do about it?"
Boy #1: "I picked up the slack."

Boy #1: "Is there Nintendo in France?"
Boy #2: "Wii."

Boy #1: "I spent a whole year learning about lumber."
Boy #2: "Where'd you go?"
Boy #1: "Boarding school."

Boy #1: "Want to hear a joke about a sheet of paper?"
Boy #2: "No way. I hear its tear-able."

Boy #1: "Want to hear a joke about an unstamped letter?"
Boy #2: "No thanks. I wouldn't get it anyway."

Girl #1: "My boyfriend lives in the house next door."
Girl #2: "So what's it like to be in a lawn-distance relationship?"

Boy #1: "I just bought a book
on anti-gravity."
Boy #2: "Was it good?"
Boy #1: "I couldn't put it down."

Boy #1: "I bought a wooden whistle, but I had to return it."
Boy #2: "Why?"
Boy #1: "It wooden whistle."

Girl #1: "My little sister threw her wooden shoes in the bathtub."
Girl #2: "So what happened?"
Girl #1: "She clogged the drain."

Boy #1: "I think I'm going to invent a pencil with an eraser at both ends."
Boy #2: "But what would be the point?"

Girl #1: "I never buy stuff that has Velcro."
Girl #2: "Why not?"
Girl #1: "Because to me it looks like a total rip-off."

Girl #1: "Have you heard about the new state-of-the-art brooms?"
Girl #2: "Yeah, I hear they're sweeping the nation."

Boy #1: "There's a man down on Main Street who's handing out dead batteries."
Boy #2: "Who wants dead batteries?"
Boy #1: "Plenty of people. All his batteries are free of charge."

Girl #1: "I really want one of those reversible jackets."
Girl #2: "Why?"
Girl #1: "I want to see how it turns out."

Boy #1: "What does the word 'coincidence' mean?"
Boy #2: "Funny, I was just going to ask you the same thing!"

Girl #1: "My phone takes photos without anybody touching it."
Girl #2: "How?"
Girl #1: "All by itselfie."

Boy #1: "My screwdriver is sick."
Boy #2: "How can you tell?"
Boy #1: "It took a turn for the worse."

Boy #1: "My uncle used to work at a bank, but he got fired."
Boy #2: "What happened?"
Boy #1: "He lost interest."

26
FUN WITH ELEPHANTS

Why are elephants so wrinkled?

They're too big to fit on an ironing board.

What do you get if you give
your elephant a pogo stick?
Big holes in your driveway.

What do you call an elephant
that refuses to take a bath?
A smellyphant.

How do you make an elephant float?
**With two scoops of ice cream,
a bottle of root beer, and an elephant.**

What would you have if Batman and Robin
were run over by a herd of elephants?
Flatman and Ribbon.

Which elephants live in Antarctica?
The cold ones.

What weighs 6,000 pounds
and wears glass slippers?
Cinderelephant.

How do you keep an elephant from charging?
Take away his credit card!

How many elephants can fit into an empty closet?
Only one. After that, the closet isn't empty anymore.

Man: "I rode an elephant to work today."
Lady: "Surely you must be joking."
Man: "I'm not joking, and please
don't call me Shirley."

When can three elephants stand under
a small umbrella and not get wet?
When it's not raining.

How do you get down from an elephant?
You don't. You get down from a duck.

When does an elephant weigh
the same as a mouse?
When the scale is broken.

What do you call an elephant that flies?
A jumbo jet.

What time is it when an elephant
sits on your watch?
Time to get a new watch.

How do you fit five elephants into a Volkswagen?
**Two in the front seat. Two in the back seat.
And one in the glove compartment.**

What's the best thing to give
a seasick elephant?

Plenty of room.

What is as big as an elephant
but weighs nothing?

Its shadow!

How does an elephant get down from a tree?

He sits on a leaf and waits for the fall.

What do you call an elephant
that doesn't matter?

An irrelephant.

27
BUZZING AROUND WITH BEES

What do you call a bee that
can't make up its mind?

A maybe.

Why are A's like flowers?

Because bees come after them.

How does a bee defend himself?

With a bee bee gun.

What kind of bee is always falling down in the hive?

A stumble-bee.

What kind of suit does a bee wear to work?

A buzzness suit.

Why do bees have sticky hair?

Because they use honey combs!

Why do bees hum?

Because they don't know the words.

What kind of haircuts do bees get?

Buzz cuts.

How do bees communicate in the hive?

They use buzzwords.

What did the bee say when it returned to the hive?

"Honey, I'm home!"

What did the bee name his son?

Buzz.

Where did Noah keep his bees?

In the Ark hives.

Which bees are best at aerial photography?

Drones.

Which insects are bad at football?

Fumble-bees.

What's the best bee for your health?

Vitamin bee.

Why do bees itch?

Because they have hives.

28

FUNNY VACATIONS

Where does a frugal bird go on vacation?

To a cheep hotel.

Traveler: "I'd like to buy a round-trip ticket."
Ticket Salesman: "Sorry. We only have square tickets."

Where do viruses go on vacation?
Germ-any.

Why did the crook take a bath
before he went on vacation?
He wanted to make a clean getaway.

Where do eggs like to go on vacation?
New Yolk City.

Where did the sheep go on vacation?
The Baaaahamas.

Where do math teachers like to go on vacation?

Times Square.

Where do the fish like to go on vacation?

Finland.

Grandma #1: "My grandkids flew all the way from California to spend a week with me."
Grandma #2: "Did you meet them at the airport?"
Grandma #1: "No, I've known them for years."

Why did the baby kangaroo hate going on vacation?

He was a pouch potato.

Where do pencils go on vacation?

Pencil-vania.

Where do locks go on vacation?

Key West.

Where do crayons go on vacation?

Color-ado.

Girl #1: "I can't wait to go on vacation.
I'm going to Africa."
Girl #2: "When are you leaving?"
Girl #1: "I'm Ghana go next week."

Where do termites like to go on vacation?

Hollywood.

Traveler #1: "Whatever you do, don't
take Peter Pan Airlines."
Traveler #2: "Why?"
Traveler #1: "They Neverland!"

The librarians chartered a plane to go on vacation, but some of them got kicked off because the flight was overbooked.

Vacationer: "I'd like a single room."
Hotel Clerk: "Would you like it with a shower or a bathtub?"
Vacationer: "I always like to save money. So what's the difference?"
Hotel Clerk: "In the shower you stand up."

Why did the elephant have a bad vacation?
Because he forgot to pack his trunk.

Girl #1: "Some day I want to go to Bora Bora."
Girl #2: "Why don't you go now?"
Girl #1: "I'm too pora pora."

Why did the coffee have such a short vacation?

On the first day it got mugged.

Traveler #1: "I sued the airline
for misplaced luggage."
Traveler #2: "What happened?"
Traveler #1: "I lost my case."

Where do bees like to go on vacation?

Stingapore.

What's brown, hairy, and wears sunglasses?

A coconut on vacation!

29

FUN WITH THE FAMILY

Mom: "Why didn't you take the school bus home?"
Son: "I tried, but it wouldn't fit into my backpack."

Boy #1: "My uncle is so rich he has two swimming pools, but one of them stays empty."
Boy #2: "Why?"
Boy #1: "It's for the people who can't swim."

Why do mothers carry babies?
Because babies can't carry mothers.

Husband: "What are we having for dinner?"
Wife: "I cooked hundreds of things."
Husband: "That's great! What did you cook?"
Wife: "Beans."

What did the little boy do
for his wonderful mother?
He built her a mom-u-ment.

Boy #1: "I remember everything about my uncle who worked in a butcher shop. He was six feet tall, wore size eleven shoes, had a forty-inch waist, and was bald."

Boy #2: "So what did he weigh?"

Boy #1: "Meat."

Boy #1: "My great-grandfather kept warning everybody that the Titanic was going to sink."

Boy #2: "What happened?"

Boy #1: "First they tried not to listen. Then they got mad. Finally, they kicked him out of the theater."

Son: "I hate alphabet soup."

Mother: "Why?"

Son: "I don't want anybody putting words in my mouth."

Dad: "I'm going to wash the car with our son."

Mom: "Couldn't you just use a sponge?"

When does a joke
become a dad joke?

When it's fully groan.

Old Woman: "You said you'd spend the rest of your life trying to make me happy."

Old Man: "I didn't expect you to live this long."

Boy #1: "I just found out they buried my great-great uncle in the wrong cemetery."

Boy #2: "That was a grave mistake."

A man had two sons,
and he named both of them Ed. Why?

Because two Eds are better than one.

Boy #1: "Until yesterday, I never knew my grandmother had false teeth."

Boy #2: "How did you find out?"

Boy #1: "I went over to her house, and it came out in the conversation."

Boy #1: "My crazy uncle finally got out of his rocking chair, but it took him ten years to do it."
Boy #2: "Wow! Your uncle must be off his rocker."

Boy #1: "My mother gave me a long list of odd jobs."
Boy #2: "So how did it turn out?"
Boy #1: "Great. I did jobs 1, 3, 5, 7, and 9."

Boy #1: "My lazy uncle just got fired from the calendar company."
Boy #2: "Why'd they fire him?"
Boy #1: "He took a couple of days off."

Patient: "Doctor, I've got a huge problem. My wife thinks she's a duck."
Doctor: "You must bring her in to see me immediately!"
Patient: "I can't. She's already flown south for the winter."

Wife: "Doctor, my husband thinks he's an elevator."
Doctor: "Tell him to come in."
Wife: "That won't work. He doesn't
stop on this floor."

Boy #1: "My uncle got robbed. Somebody stole
every lamp in his house."
Boy #2: "So how's he taking it?"
Boy #1: "He's de-lighted."

Boy #1: "My crazy uncle tried to cross the
English Channel on a plank, but he gave up."
Boy #2: "What happened?"
Boy #1: "He couldn't find a plank
that was long enough."

Boy #1: "Our dog is just like
a member of our family."
Boy #2: "Which one?"

30

CRAZY CATS AND FUNNY FELINES

What is a cat's favorite movie?

The Sound of Mew-sic!

What kind of cars do cats drive?

Catillacs!

What did the alien say to the cat?

"Take me to your litter."

Where do cats go to look at famous paintings?

The mewseum.

What does a cat have that no other animal has?

Kittens.

What do you call a man who got attacked by a cat?

Claude.

Which cats make the best bowlers?

Alley cats.

What did the baseball-playing cat
say when he struck out?

"Me-out."

What do invisible cats drink?

Evaporated milk.

What do baby cats wear?

Diapurrrrs.

Cat #1: "How did you do in the
milk-drinking contest?"
Cat #2: "I won by five laps."

How do you get a cat to fetch a stick?

Put a dog in a cat suit.

How do cats end a fight?

They hiss and make up.

Why do cats scratch themselves?

Because nobody else knows where the itch is.

How did the kitten do in school?

Purrrrfect. It was the teacher's pet.

Why was the kitten in a bad mood?

It needed a catnap.

When is it bad luck to have
a black cat cross your path?

When you're a mouse.

What do cats like to eat for dessert?

Mice cream.

What do you call a huge pile of cats?

A meowtain.

What happened to the cat
who swallowed the ball of wool?

She had mittens.

31

LET'S LAUGH ABOUT THE WEATHER

What do clouds wear in their hair?

Rainbows.

What do you call a warm snowman?

Water.

What is at the end of a rainbow?

The letter W.

What did the raincloud name his daughter?

Misty.

What happened to the wind?

It blew away.

How do hurricanes see?

With one eye.

What does a cloud wear under his raincoat?

Thunderwear.

What color is rain?

Water color.

What goes up when the rain comes down?

An umbrella.

What's the difference between
weather and climate?

You can't weather a tree, but you can climate.

What's the difference between
a horse and a storm?

One is reined in and the other rains down.

Where do snowmen dance?
At the snowball.

What lives in the winter, grows upside down,
and dies in the summer?

An icicle.

What kind of umbrella does the mayor
of New York use on a rainy day?

A wet one.

I tried to catch some fog.

I mist.

Boy #1: "During the middle of the summer our
town got hit by a snowstorm."
Boy #2: "What happened?"
Boy #1: "The weatherman said it was an ice-olated
event."

What do you call a warm iceberg?

The ocean.

Knock, knock.
Who's there?
Wayne.
Wayne who?

**Wayne, Wayne, go away.
Come again some other day.**

Boy #1: "Did you hear the news about the smog?"
Boy #2: "You don't have to tell me.
It's all over town."

What is every snowman's favorite cereal?

Frosted Flakes.

What kind of person adds best in hot weather?

A summer.

What do you call a weatherman who works
a second job at a butcher shop?

A meat-eorologist.

What did the dirt say to the rain?

"If you keep this up, my name will be mud."

Why can't it rain for two nights in a row?

Because there's a day in between.

What did summer say to spring?

"Help, I'm going to fall!"

What did the breeze say to the window screen?

"Just passing through."

32

LAUGHING WITH THE MONKEYS AND THE APES

What do you call a baby monkey?

A chimp off the old block.

Where do gorillas like to work out?

The jungle gym.

Why don't monkeys play cards in the jungle?

There are too many cheetahs there.

Why did the monkey eat so many bananas?

He liked them a bunch.

Why does a baby monkey walk softly?

Because it's a baby, and it can't walk, hardly.

What do you call two monkeys sharing an Amazon
account?

PRIME-mates.

What is the monkey's favorite cookie?
Chocolate chimp.

What did the chimpanzee say when
he found out his sister had a baby?
"Well, I'll be a monkey's uncle."

Why are monkeys such terrible storytellers?
Because they only have one tail.

What does a gorilla wear when it cooks?
An ape-eron.

Why don't monkeys like to walk down stairs?
Because they'd rather slide down the banana-ster.

What do you call a gorilla who plays golf?
Hairy Putter.

What do you call a monkey who
eats a ton of potato chips?
A chipmunk.

What did the chimp eat before dinner?
An ape-etizer.

What's a gorilla's favorite fruit?
Ape-ri-cot.

What's the easiest way to catch a monkey?
Climb a tree and act like a banana.

What do you call a monkey that's
sitting on the North Pole?
Lost.

33
LET'S GO OUT TO EAT AND LET'S LAUGH!

Customer: "Waiter, my food tastes funny."
Waiter: "Then why aren't you laughing?"

Man: "Do you serve lobsters?"
Waiter: "Of course. We serve anybody."

Customer: "Waiter, there's a fly in my soup."
Waiter: "Don't worry. The frog will surface soon."

Man: "Waiter, there's a fly in my soup!"
Waiter: "Don't worry. The spider underneath your bread is about to take care of it."

Customer: "Waiter, this coffee tastes like mud!"
Waiter: "I'm not surprised. A year ago, it was ground."

Man: "Waiter, there's a bee in my soup."
Waiter: "Of course there is. You ordered alphabet soup."

Man: "Waiter, I don't like all the flies in here."
Waiter: "Then come back tomorrow. We'll have some new ones by then."

Customer: "I'd like a cup of coffee, without cream."
Waiter: "I'm sorry, we're out of cream.
Would you like it without milk?"

Waiter: "How do you like your steak?"
Man: "It's horrible. I won't eat it.
Please get your manager."
Waiter: "It's no use. He won't eat it, either."

Customer: "Waiter, what's this fly
doing in my soup?"
Waiter: "It looks to me like
he's doing the backstroke."

Teddy Bear: "That meal was great."
Waiter: "I'm glad. Would you like dessert?"
Teddy Bear: "No thanks. I'm stuffed."

Man: "Will my pizza be long?
Waiter: "No, it will be round."

34

MORE FUN WITH FOOD

Boy #1: "Your sundae is a mess. What happened?"

Boy #2: "The banana split and the ice screamed."

Mother: "Did you eat all the cookies
in the cookie jar?"
Little Boy: "No, I didn't touch one."
Mother: "Then why is there only one left?"
Little Boy: "That's the one I didn't touch!"

Mom: "Why is there an egg on the front porch
and an egg on the back porch?"
Girl: "The recipe said, 'Separate two eggs.'"

Man #1: "I hear you're about to start a bakery."
Man #2: "That's right. I'm going to open it up as
soon as I can raise the dough."

When is the best time to eat a banana?
After it's peeled.

Why did the vegetable band break up?
It didn't have a beet.

What does a gingerbread man put on his bed?

A cookie sheet.

What do you call rotten eggs, spoiled fruit, and curdled milk mixed up in a brown bag?

Gross-eries.

Which is the most adorable vegetable?

The cute-cumber.

What kind of nut doesn't have a shell?

A doughnut.

How do you make an egg roll?

You give it a push.

What did the ham do when he wanted
to talk to the pot roast?

He called a meat-ing.

What did the potato chip say to the nacho chip?

"Want to go for a dip?"

What does ice cream wear to church?

It's sundae best.

What does a fruit say when he apologizes?

"I'm berry sorry."

Who invented the steak?

Sir Loin.

How do you turn a bowl
of soup into gold?
Just add 24 carrots.

Why did the little potato cry in the bathtub?

He got soap in his eyes.

What happens to a green bean
if you throw it into the Red Sea?

It gets wet.

What starts with T, ends with T, and is full of T?

A teapot.

What did Mr. and Mrs. Hamburger
name their daughter?

Patty.

What's the coolest food?

Chili.

Why did the orange put on sunblock?

Because it was starting to peel.

What do beavers eat for breakfast?

Oakmeal.

What did the cook name his baby boy?

Stew.

Why is breakfast the funniest meal?

Because the egg always cracks a yoke.

Why did all the onions get together at a state park?

They wanted to have a family re-onion.

Why was the ice cube so smart?

It had 32 degrees.

What is a statue's favorite dessert?

Marble cake.

Why did the woman decide to
hide her money in the freezer?

Because she wanted some cold, hard cash.

What's orange and sounds like a parrot?

A carrot.

How do pickles enjoy a day off work?
They relish it.

What did the cucumber say to the pickle?
"You mean a great dill to me."

When do you stop at green and go at red?
When you're eating a watermelon.

What did the hamburger give to his girlfriend?
An onion ring.

What fruit do scarecrows love the most?
Strawberries.

What fruit never wants to be alone?

A pear.

What do you call a runaway pea?

An esc-a-pea.

What did the plate say to the water glass?

"Dinner's on me."

What kind of key opens a banana?

A mon-key.

What do you call a retired vegetable?

A has-bean.

What do you call a sad strawberry?

A blueberry.

What's the laziest food?

Bread. It just loafs around.

Why did the orange pull over
to the side of the road?

It ran out of juice.

How many peas are there in a pint?

There's only one P in "pint."

How do you know that peanuts are fattening?

Have you ever seen a skinny elephant?

What did the lettuce say
during the fire drill?

"Lettuce romaine calm."

If an apple a day keeps the doctor away,
what does an onion a day do?

It keeps everybody away.

What day of the week do potatoes dread?

Fry-day.

What's the funniest candy?

LOL-i-pops.

What do you call a sad cup of coffee?

A depresso.

Jokes about German sausages are the **wurst.**

If you dropped a tomato on your toe, would it hurt?

Yes, but only if it's were still in the can.

What's the healthiest kind of water?

Well water.

What do you call a pickle that thinks he's a flower?

A daffy-dill.

Why did the jelly roll?

Because it saw the apple turnover.

How can you tell if an elephant
has been in your refrigerator?

By the big footprints in the butter.

How does a hot dog speak?

Frankly.

What do you call stolen candy?

Hot chocolate.

What kind of person loves cocoa?

A coconut.

How can you scramble an egg without breaking it?

Get somebody else to break it.

If you drop a pumpkin from a tall building,
what is it by the time it hits the ground?

Squash.

How does a coffee pot feel when it's hot?
Perky.

What is a whistling teapot's favorite song?
"Home on the Range."

With which vegetable do you throw away the outside, cook the inside, eat the other outside, and throw away the other inside?
Corn on the cob.

What did the pot do with the chili's secret?
It spilled the beans.

Why did the potato chip stop the car and get out?
Because it saw a dip in the road.

How do you get an entire cow
to fit into a frying pan?
Use shortening.

What do you call a knife that cuts
four loaves of bread at the same time?
A four-loaf cleaver.

Why was the teacher so disappointed
with the gallon of milk?
It only gave 2%.

Why did the chocolate candy
get suspended from school?
Because it fudged on the exam.

What bakery treat tried to rule the world?
Atilla the Bun.

Boy #1: "My sister bet me I couldn't build a car out of spaghetti."
Boy #2: "What happened?"
Boy #1: "You should have seen her face when I drove pasta."

Boy #1: "I've decided to become a vegetarian."
Boy #2: "I think that's a big missed steak."

Mother: "I'm sorry, but I only know how to make three dishes: meat loaf, scrambled eggs, and apple pie."
Daughter: "Which one is this?"

The cookbook we'd all like to see:

"100 Ways to Cook a Hot Dog"
By Frank Furter

35
CRAZY RIDDLES ABOUT ANIMALS

How do you start a turtle race?

"Ready, set, slow!"

Where do mice park their boats?

At the hickory dickory dock.

What is a bunny's favorite music?

Hip-hop.

What do you call a bear with no teeth?

A gummy bear!

What do you call a thieving alligator?

A crookodile.

What is the snake's favorite subject?

Hiss-story.

What do you get when you train your chicken to wake you up every morning?

An alarm cluck.

Why did the policeman give the sheep a ticket?

He was a baaaaaaaaad driver.

What is more amazing than a talking horse?

A spelling bee.

Why can't a snake ever win an argument?

Because it doesn't have a leg to stand on.

Why did the police arrest the snail?

Because he was found at the scene of the slime.

What do you get when you
cross a shellfish and a rabbit?

The Oyster Bunny.

Which animal can't stop talking during class?

A yak.

What do you call an easy-going rabbit?

Hoppy-go-lucky.

What do you call a snake who
works for the government?

A civil serpent.

Why couldn't the pony sing?

Because she was a little hoarse.

What happened when the frog
broke down on the highway?

He got toad away.

Why do mother kangaroos hate rainy days?

Because their children have to play inside.

What did the tired horse do at night?

It hit the hay.

What kind of medicine do ants take?

Ant-i-biotics.

What did the mother chameleon say to
her nervous child on the first day of school?

"Don't worry. You'll blend right in."

What did the round bunny say to the square bunny?

"You're not from a round hare."

Where do funny frogs sit?

On silly pads.

Where do squirrels go before kindergarten?

Tree school.

What kind of school does a giraffe go to?

High school.

What's the scariest horse in the world?

A nightmare.

What do you give an alligator
when it gets hurt?

Gatorade.

What did the frog order for lunch?

French flies and a large croak.

How long was the hamster's workout?

Wheel-ie long.

What do you give a pig with a rash?

Oinkment.

Why is it so hard to have a conversation with a goat?

Because the goat keeps butting in.

Which state do dogs, cats,
hamsters, and canaries like best?

Petsylvania.

What is every mouse's favorite letter?

It's the letter S because it makes a cat scat.

What did the horse say after he finished
eating the bale of hay?

"That's the last straw!"

Where to donkeys hang their artwork?

In a museum.

What do you call a kangaroo that raps?

A hip hopper.

What should you do if your sheep gets sick?

Call a lambulance.

Where do butterflies sleep?

On cater-pillows.

Where do polar bears go to vote?

The north poll.

What do you get if you cross
a snake and a LEGO set?

A boa constructor.

Why are frogs always so happy?

Because they eat whatever bugs them.

What do you call a pig who
turns to a life of crime?
A ham-burglar.

How do you make an octopus laugh?
You give him ten-tickles.

What did the horse say when
he had nothing to eat but thistles?
"Thistle have to do."

What do you call a lost wolf?
A where-wolf.

Why did the spider move away from home?
It wanted to change websites.

How do you find out where
a bug has bitten you?
You've got to start from scratch.

What do you call a flying rabbit?
A hareplane.

How does a polar bear build his house?
Igloos it together.

36
LAUGHING AROUND THE HOUSE

What kind of house weighs the least?

A lighthouse.

What kind of room has no windows,
no doors, and no walls?

A mushroom.

What does a broom do at night?

It goes to sweep.

When is a door not a door?

When it's ajar.

If a red house is made of red bricks
and a blue house is made of blue bricks,
what is a green house made of?

Glass.

What kind of clothing does a house wear?

An address.

What did one wall say to the other wall?

"I'll meet you at the corner."

What did the carpet say to the ceiling?

"I've always looked up to you."

A man walks into a room with a fireplace,
a wood stove, and a kerosene lamp.
What should he light first?

A match.

Why was the broom late?

It over swept.

What has one head, one foot, and four legs?

A bed.

What did the alien say to the lawnmower?

"Take me to your weeder."

What invention allows you to look through walls?

A window.

What do you call a flower
that keeps coming back?

A bloomerang.

What did the rug name his son?

Mat.

What did the blanket say to the bed?

"Don't worry. I've got you covered."

What gets answered but never asks a question?
A doorbell.

Why did the Scottish man
have plumbing problems?
Because he only had bagpipes.

What did the big chimney
say to the little chimney?
"You're too young to smoke."

What's blue and smells like red paint?
Blue paint.

How can you fall off a 100-foot
ladder without getting hurt?
That's easy. Just fall off the bottom rung.

What do you call an educated hole in the wall?

A wise crack.

What happens to a refrigerator
when you pull its plug?

It becomes uncool.

Why was the door so nervous?

It was unhinged.

How can you tell when your
dirty dishes are in trouble?

They're in hot water.

What did the painter say to the wall?

**"One more crack like that and
I'm going to plaster you."**

What do you call a man who puts
his mattress in the chandelier?

A light sleeper.

Boy #1: "I decided to sell my vacuum cleaner."
Boy #2: "Why?"
Boy #1: "All it was doing was gathering dust."

Wife: "I hate to tell you this, but there's
a wash basin in front of our door right now."
Husband: "Can you give me a minute
to let that sink in?"

37
HAPPY HOLIDAYS!

What do Santa's elves do after school?

Their gnomework.

Why does Santa like going down the chimney?
Because it soots him.

What is a parent's favorite Christmas carol?
Silent Night.

What nationality is Santa Claus?
North Polish.

What is Tarzan's favorite Christmas carol?
Jungle Bells.

Why does Santa have a garden?
So he can hoe, hoe, hoe!

What do you call a pumpkin
that thinks he's a comedian?

A joke-a-lantern.

Why is it cold on Christmas day?

Because it's in Decembrrrrrrrr!

What is Santa's favorite kind of music?

Gift rap.

What disease can you get from putting up
too many Christmas decorations?

Tinselitus.

Why couldn't the elf pay his rent?

Because he was a little short.

What does Frosty the Snowman
put in his coffee?

Cold cream.

Where does Santa go to buy his potatoes?

Idaho-ho-ho.

How do you fix a jack-o-lantern?

With a pumpkin patch.

Why doesn't St. Nicholas like to shave?

**Because every time he does,
the saint nicks himself.**

What do birds give out on Halloween?

Tweets.

What do you call Santa when he stops moving?

Santa Pause.

What is a cow's favorite holiday?

Moo Year's Eve.

What do you call someone who
plays tricks on Halloween?

Prankenstein.

If the Pilgrims were alive today,
what would they be most famous for?

Their age.

What did the light bulb say to
his girlfriend on Valentine's Day?

"I love you watts and watts."

Why are masks always worth less
on the day after Halloween?
Because they've lost their face value.

What do elves learn in school?
The elf-a-bit.

Knock, knock.
Who's there?
Murray.
Murray who?
Murry Christmas to all and to all good night.

What do you call the fear of Santa Claus?
Claustrophobia.

38

AND FINALLY: A FEW MORE LAUGHS BEFORE YOU GO

What did one calculator say
to the other calculator?

"You can count on me."

Why did the scientist remove his doorbell?
He wanted to win the no-bell prize.

Why do squirrels spend so
much time up in the trees?
To get away from all the nuts on the ground.

Who wears the smallest hat?
A narrow-minded person.

After the French cheese factory collapsed,
all that was left was de Brie.

What is taken before you get it?
Your picture.

What's the hottest part of a man's face?
His sideburns.

How do knights change channels?
With a remoat.

What's a magician's favorite cereal?
Trix.

What side of a campfire is the hottest?
The fireside.

What's the best way to communicate with a Viking?
Norse Code.

What was the greatest invention in history?

The wheel because it got everything rolling.

What happens to all the pennies
that people throw into fountains?

They get wet.

What happened to the boy
who ran away with the circus?

**Eventually his mother found him
and made him take it back.**

Who is bigger: Mrs. Bigger or her baby?

Her baby is a little Bigger.

My friend borrowed my grandfather clock.
He owes me big time.

Who earns a living by driving his customers away?
An Uber driver.

What is purple and is 10,000 miles long?
The Grape Wall of China.

Rule #1 for Scientists: If you're doing a science
experiment, don't lick the spoon.

What do you get if you cross
a snowman with an alligator?
Frostbite.

What has a head but can't think and drives but can't steer?

A hammer.

Girl #1: "A burglar broke into
the wig shop last night."
Girl #2: "That's terrible.
What are the police doing about it?"
Girl #1: "They are combing the area."

Who has the strongest fingers in the world?
The miser because he's always pinching pennies.

Two antennae got married.
The ceremony was dull, but the reception was great.

Who did Antarctica marry?
Uncle Arctica.

Why was the little shoe so sad?
**Because his father was a loafer
and his mother was a sneaker.**

If a boomerang comes back to you,
why throw it in the first place?

Why did the robot win the dance contest?
Because he was a dancing machine.

Why couldn't Humpty Dumpty
be put back together again?
Because he wasn't all he was cracked up to be.

Dry-erase boards are remarkable.

What runs around all day and then lies under the bed all night with its tongue hanging out?

Your shoe.

Did you hear about the strongman who picked up an entire store?

He was a shoplifter.

Why did the man sing in the shower?

He wanted to be in a soap opera.

Why did Paul Revere give away his handkerchief?

Because he bumped into the town crier.

Boy #1: "The man at the ice rink only charges a dollar an hour."
Boy #2: "That's a cheap skate."

What did the cheerful light bulb
say to the sad light bulb?
"You need to lighten up."

What do you call the rear entrance of a cafeteria?
A bacteria.

Man #1: "For years I thought I was a flamingo,
but I finally got over it."
Man #2: "How did you do it?"
Man #1: "I finally put my foot down."

Why is a room full of married couples empty?
Because there's not a single person in it.

What do chairs use to hold up their pants?
Seat belts.

What is the difference between a
greedy person and an electric toaster?

One takes the most and the other makes the toast.

I saw a book that promised to solve 50%
of my problems, so I bought two copies.

Why do you always start
walking with your right foot?

**Because when you move one foot,
the other one is left-behind.**

What did one candle say to the other candle?

"Are you going out tonight?"

Is it better to write on a full stomach
or on an empty stomach?

Neither. It's better to write on paper.

What gets wetter the more it dries?

A towel.

How do you go without sleep
for seven days and not get tired?

Sleep at night.

Man #1: "I asked my tailor to make
me a new pair of pants."
Man #2: "What did he say?"
Man #1: "He seemed happy to do it,
or sew it seams."

What has one foot on each side
and a foot in the middle?

A yardstick.

Why are identical twins like
two broken alarm clocks?

Because they are dead ringers.

What is full of holes and can still hold water?

A sponge.

What is always behind the times?

The backside of clock.

They had a funeral for the
pot of water that boiled away.

It will be mist.

What's another name for a grandfather clock?

An old-timer.

What kind of fall makes you unconscious
but doesn't hurt you?

Falling asleep.

Boy #1: "Can you stand on your head?"
Boy #2: "I've tried, but I can't
get my feet up high enough."

What did the digital clock say
to the grandfather clock?
"Look Grandpa: no hands!"

Man: "Hello, 911, I'm calling to report an accident.
I slipped on a banana peel and fell into my TV,
which crashed through a window,
and smashed onto my car."
911 Dispatcher: "Sir, could you repeat that?"
Man: "Not if I can help it!"

Why does the Statue of Liberty
stand in New York Harbor?
Because there's no place to sit.

What do Alexander the Great
and
Winnie the Poo have in common?
Same middle name.

Did you hear about the burglar
who fell in the cement mixer?
Now he's a hardened criminal.

An egg floated down the Mississippi River
from Memphis to New Orleans.
Where did it come from?
From a chicken.

Boy #1: "Why are you jumping up and down?"
Boy #2: "Because I just took some medicine
but I forgot to shake the bottle."

What was purple and conquered the world?
Alexander the Grape.

What can you put in a glass put never take out of it?
A crack.

Man: "I have questions about my future."

Fortune Teller: "You've come to the right place. I charge ten dollars per question."

Man: "Isn't that a little expensive?"

Fortune Teller: "That'll be ten dollars."

What do you call a boomerang
that doesn't come back?

A bummerang.

Where can you find King Arthur
on Saturday nights?

At his favorite knight club.

Boy #1: "I got a new dog. You want to play with it?"

Boy #2: "Does it bite?"

Boy #1: "That's what I want to find out."

Why was the karate teacher
arrested at the butcher shop?

He was caught choplifting.

Why is a crossword puzzle like a silly quarrel?

**Because in both cases,
one word inevitably leads to another.**

Boy #1: "What's Tommy's last name?"
Boy #2: "Tommy who?"

What has eight feet and can sing?

A barbershop quartet.

Boy: "Here's your Christmas present:
a box of your favorite chocolates."
Girl: "But the box is half empty."
Boy: "I know. They're my favorite chocolates too."

What is heavy forward but not backwards?

Ton.

What has cities without houses, rivers without water, and forests without trees?

A map.

What speaks in every language?

An echo.

What flies when it's on and floats when it's off?

A feather.

Lady: "Why is this letter wet?"
Mailman: "There was postage dew."

Why didn't the dime play in traffic with the nickel?
Because it had more cents.

Why do all Swedish ships have bar codes?
So when they arrive in port they can Scandinavian.

What can you give away and still keep?
A cold.

Why couldn't the bicycle stand up by itself?
Because it was two tired.

How do you feel when you have lice?
Lousy.

What did nine say to six?

"Why are you standing on your head?"

Where do toilet paper rolls sleep?

Under the sheets.

What do you call a belt with a built-in clock?

A waist of time.

Why did the candle get sent to its room?

It had a meltdown.

What do you call a boomerang
that doesn't come back?

A stick!

Why did the painting go to jail?
Because it got framed.

How come the Tin Man never took a bath?
He was always squeaky clean.

What runs but can't walk?
The faucet.

Why can you never believe what an atom says?
Because they make up everything.

How did the cowboy burn his bottom?
He rode the range.

Who went to jail for stealing
soap out of the bathtub?

The Robber Ducky.

When you're looking for something, why does it
always seem to be in the last place you look?

Because once you find it, you stop looking.

Where does Superman get the food he needs
to leap tall buildings in a single bound?

At the Super-Market.

In the jailhouse, what is every
prisoner's favorite celebration?

A going-away party.

What's the difference between
an ice cream cone and a bully?
One you lick and the other licks you.

Why don't you wear a cardboard belt?
That would be a waist of paper.

Why are shoemakers such kind people?
Because they have good soles.

If George Washington were alive today,
why couldn't he throw a silver dollar
across the Potomac River?
Because a dollar doesn't go as far as it used to.

Did you hear about the fire at the circus?
The heat was in-tents.

Why is an airplane pilot like a football player?
They both want to make safe touchdowns.

Why did Miss Muppet buy a map?
Because she lost her whey.

What kind of car does
Mickey Mouse's girlfriend drive?
A Minnie van.

What are the three fastest means of
communication?
Telephone, telegraph, and tell-a-secret.

What happens when you spend too
much time in the sun reading a book?
You're well red.

How could you tell it was an emotional wedding?

Even the cake was in tiers.

What's the difference between
a man and a running dog?

One wears trousers and the other pants.

What do you get if you cross
a jumbo jet with a kangaroo?

A plane that makes short hops.

Why did it take four boy scouts to help
just one old lady across the road?

Because she didn't want to go.

Why did Humpty Dumpty have a great fall?

To make up for a lousy summer.

Why did the boy cut a hole
in the top of his umbrella?
So he could see when it stopped raining.

What has a tongue but never talks,
and has no legs but sometim≥es walks?
A shoe.

Why did the man put his pants on backwards?
Because he didn't know if he was coming or going.

What do you call a yo-yo without a string?
A no-yo.

It's a container without hinges or a key,
but it has golden treasure inside. What is it?
An egg.

What did Paul Revere say when he finished his midnight ride?

"Whoa!"

What do you call a fast tricycle?

A tot rod.

What did the blanket say
to the stack of unpaid bills?

"Don't worry. I'll cover all your expenses."

Why was the screw so mad?

Because it didn't get its turn.

What goes around the corner but never moves?

A road.

What did one penny say to the other penny?

"We make perfect cents."

Why is England so damp and wet?

Because the queen had a very long reign.

What's the oiliest place on Earth?

Greece.

Where does the queen keep her dogs?

In Barkingham Palace.

Why did the ballerina decide to quit dancing?

Because it was tutu hard.

What lies on the bottom of the ocean and fidgets?

A nervous wreck.

Where do police officers like to meet for lunch?

At the arrestaurant.

What is a snowman's favorite food?

An iceburger.

What do you call dirt that isn't real?

Play ground.

Who invented the first plane that wouldn't fly?

The Wrong Brothers.

Why did the king do so well in school?

He liked all his subjects.

Where does a power cord prefer to shop?

At the outlet mall.

The penny and the nickel decided to go cliff diving.
So why didn't the quarter go along with the crowd?

The quarter had more cents.

What did George Washington tell his troops
before they crossed the Delaware?

"Get in the boat."

Which tower is never hungry?

The I-Full Tower.

What do you call a phone that won't share?
Cellfish.

What do you call somebody who's
always washing his hands?
The Germinator.

How does a clock put its gloves on?
One hand at a time.

What's the perfect cure for dandruff?
Baldness.

What is round and has a really bad temper?
A vicious cycle.

Where do belly buttons go after high school?
The Navel Academy.

Why are country people smarter than city people?
Because in big cities, the population is denser.

What did the Eskimo say when
he returned to his igloo?
"There's snow place like home."

How did the big mountain know
the little mountain was lying?
Because it was obviously just a bluff.

What's the best way to avoid biting insects?
Promise yourself that you'll never bite them.

What kind of driver never gets a ticket?

A screwdriver.

Which runs faster, hot or cold?

Hot. Anybody can catch a cold.

Why did the man run around his bed?

Because he was trying to catch up on his sleep!

What stays in the corner
but travels all over the world?

A stamp.

Wife: "You've got your pants on inside out."
Husband: "I know, but there are holes
on the other side."

What happened after Jack broke his crown?

Everything went downhill after that.

Dancer #1: "I used to be addicted
to the Hokey Pokey."
Dancer #2: "How did you get over it?"
Dancer #1: "Finally, I was able to turn myself
around."

Mother: "What did your father
say after he fell in the lake?"
Son: "Do you want me to leave
out the bad words?"
Mother: "Yes."
Son: "He didn't say anything."